Teacher's Guide

The Mighty Works of God

SELF GOVERNMENT

A Child's History of the United States of America

Ruth J. Smith

ACKNOWLEDGMENTS

Many years of study and teaching are represented in this work designed to restore to the children of America the record of God's mighty work in bringing forth this nation. The accomplishment of the project could not have been reached without the help and encouragement of family and friends.

The work is dedicated to my grandchildren, Cari, Courtney, John, Jonathan, Chad, Christina, Kaylynn, and Beth. Their eagerness to learn was the inspiration to produce the work that had been in my heart and mind for many years. My prayer is that this work will be not only for my grandchildren, but for the children and children's children in many families and the students in many classrooms, who will enjoy learning of God's work in the lives of men and nations.

What a blessing it has been to labor with my three daughters in producing this work. I cannot begin to name all that Mrs. Lynn Meier, Mrs. Jeanette Whittaker, and Mrs. Charlene Trowbridge have sacrificially given to make this work a reality. Many hours in editing, sharing ideas which they have used in the classroom, assisting in designing the volume and the student materials are only the tip of the iceberg. Their labor of love does not go unnoticed.

My son-in-law, Craig Trowbridge, deserves my thanks for his patient assistance in serving as a computer consultant, and his contribution in the production of the resource CD.

I want to express my heartfelt thanks to Mrs. Lisa Mikler, who shared the vision of the volume and invested countless hours to illustrate the content of the volume in a manner consistent with the ideas presented. The delightful pictures enhance the book and bring the historic events to life.

The publication of this work could never have been accomplished without the prayers and funding of individuals and foundations who recognized the need for a Providential history for children. My appreciation is extended to these friends, including the following:

American Christian Education
    Foundation
Mr. and Mrs. Lee Kilmer
Mr. and Mrs. John Kinzer
Lighthouse Foundation
Mr. and Mrs. Don McNeill
Mr. and Mrs. David Olson
Possibility Christian School
Mr. and Mrs. Robert Thompson
Rhema Foundation
Mr. and Mrs. James Rose
Mr. and Mrs. Thomas Vedrenne
Mr. and Mrs. Allen Whittaker
Mr. and Mrs. William Wood

Miss Katherine Dang, President of Philomath Foundation, long-time friend and associate, graciously took time from her research and writing in Universal History, to edit the first chapters of the Student Text. Her consistent support and wise counsel are gratefully appreciated.

I want to thank Mr. James Rose, President of American Christian History Institute, associate for many years, for his advancement of the ideas for teaching America's Christian History in the elementary classroom through *A Guide to American Christian Education for the Home and School*, the classic work on American Christian education, published in 1987. This first published expression is the foundation on which this work has been built. For these many years, Mr. Rose has encouraged the teaching and expansion of that work.

These acknowledgements would not be complete without recognizing the faithful encouragement given by my husband, Allen Smith, as we labored together in the ministry of preserving America's Providential history and restoring American Christian education, through the Pilgrim Institute ministry. Though no longer with us in body, I know he would rejoice to see the publication of this volume.

My heart's desire in publishing this work is that American Christians will be prepared to teach the children of the next generation the Mighty Works of God, that the next generation will have the character to remember His works, and that there might be a *healing* in our land. "That the generations to come might know *them*, *even* the children which should be born; *who* should arise and declare *them* to their children: That they might set their hope in God, and not forget the works of God, but keep his commandments." Psalm 78:7-8.

— Ruth J. Smith

TABLE OF CONTENTS

Part IV—APPENDIX

PREFACE

This volume, the first in a series for elementary children, began about 1972. My husband and I attended a class at our church in which we were introduced to the idea that America had a Christian history. My education had included many history courses, whose facts had been promptly forgotten, but none which brought me to recognize the Biblical truth of God's Providential direction in the lives of men and *nations*.

This class began a journey of learning which revolutionized our lives and home. As we studied the Biblical principles of government which formed the United States of America, we recognized that these principles had both individual and national application. The primary historical works which guided this journey were *The Christian History of the Constitution of the United States of America,* by Verna M. Hall, and its companion volume, *Teaching and Learning America's Christian History,* by Rosalie J. Slater.

As my heart and life changed, the Lord opened doors in the field of education, first in the classroom with students, and later teaching adults.

In the Christian school classroom, it soon became apparent that most teaching materials were simply a study of dates, facts, names, and events, with no consideration to their cause and effect. It became my desire to pass on to students the *joy* of learning America's Providential history. Rather than history being regarded as *dull* and *boring*, students could understand the *cause* of history and the individual's importance in His Story. Studying history with an effort to determine the cause and effect of events gives *life* to the subject.

Nearly 30 years ago, I accepted the challenge of developing a plan for teaching America's Christian history to children. Ideas were identified, expanded, confirmed, and taught to students and in countless workshops. In 1987, the plan was published in *A Guide to American Christian Education for the Home and School.*

In 1992, two Teacher's Guides were produced and published by Pilgrim Institute. The first was co-authored with Jeanette Smith, *An American Christian Approach for Teaching Christopher Columbus in the Primary Grades,* and the second was co-authored with Lynn Meier, *An American Christian Approach for Teaching Christopher Columbus and the Discovery of the New World.*

For more than a decade, educators in homes and classrooms expressed repeatedly the need for more detailed history materials. Thus, the arduous task of writing Student Texts and Teacher's Guides began.

Generations of children have grown to love and appreciate the unique individual liberty which has prospered in America as Christian self government was exercised, Christian character cultivated and practiced, property valued, and discernment exercised in establishing and maintaining a form of government built upon Scriptural principles.

This present work is designed to further assist families and educators who recognize the responsibility for perpetuating a nation's ideals and principles, and who desire to place before their children the story of how God uses individuals and nations to forward His Story.

—Ruth J. Smith

Part I

TEACHING AMERICA'S CHRISTIAN HISTORY IN THE ELEMENTARY SCHOOL

God commands His people to remember all He has done for them as individuals and nations (Deut. 7:18; 8:2; Joshua 4:1-9). Noah Webster stated that "to remember is to have in the mind an idea which had been in the mind before, and which recurs to the mind without effort." Indeed, as Emma Willard observed, ". . . if we expect that memory will treasure up the objects of attention," it would help to acknowledge that "Each individual is to himself the centre of his own world and the more intimately he connects his knowledge with himself, the better will it be remembered . . ."[1] Hence, if the individual rejoices upon every remembrance of the grace of God in his *personal* history and world, he errs in forgetting God's Providence—His immediate, sovereign care and supervision—in his *nation's* unique history.

Today, the study of history has become a study of dates, facts, names, and events, with no consideration for their cause and effect. This approach to history has produced students who regard history as *dull* and *boring* and who have some knowledge of *facts* (or effects) of history, but no understanding of the *cause* of history and the individual's importance in His Story. Studying history with an effort to determine the cause and effect of events gives *life* to the subject.

The individual Christian must determine what is the cause of all events in his own personal history and his nation's history. Rev. S. W. Foljambe declared a causal relationship in his Annual Election Sermon, January 5, 1876, "It has been said that history is the biography of communities; in another, and profounder, sense, it is the autobiography of him 'who worketh all things after the counsel of his own will' (Eph. 1:11), and who is graciously timing all events in the interests of his Christ, and of the kingdom of God on earth."[2]

Recognizing God as the cause of events of history will make the study of history truly Christian. How the Holy Spirit must be grieved when history is attributed to other than the true source!

A study of history from the premise that God is in control will cause the individual to recognize that God has a plan for each individual and nation. After Christ brought Christianity, Christianity through God's Divine direction moved westward with its effect in civil liberty. This westward march of Christianity produced America, the world's first Christian Republic established with a Christian form of government.

In many classrooms, history loses its identity when it is blended into a social studies course. The teaching of social

1

studies produces an individual who has no mastery of history and who has a philosophy based upon man as causative, with a great emphasis upon societies rather than the individual. As early as 1876, the Centennial of American Independence, Rev. Foljambe cautioned Americans against a failure to study Providential history: "The more thoroughly a nation deals with its history, the more decidedly will it recognize and own an overruling Providence therein, and the more religious a nation will it become; while the more superficially it deals with its history, seeing only secondary causes and human agencies, the more irreligious will it be."[3]

The failure to teach history produces an irreligious people who attribute all advancement to man's efforts. History studied from original source documents enables individuals to see God's Hand moving to fulfill His plan and purpose and to therefore give God, not man, the glory.

American Christians must *again*, as the forefathers did, recognize that America is the direct result of Christianity and its relationship to all areas of life, including the sphere of civil government. American Christians must recognize the link between internal Christian liberty and external religious and civil liberty. If the foundations of America are to be restored, these premises must become an integral part of the teacher's philosophy of history and government and thus direct how and what he teaches in the classroom.

Developing the Elementary Christian History Program

History records the evidence of God's use of individual men and nations to move Christianity westward. This westward movement produced America and her Christian form of government.

The Mighty Works of God: Self Government identifies nine major links used by God to move Christianity westward.

In *The Christian History of the Constitution of the United States of America*, historian Verna Hall identified individuals, events, and nations, used of God, to bring forth America and her form of government. These nine links were derived from that work.[4]

Christianity Moved Westward

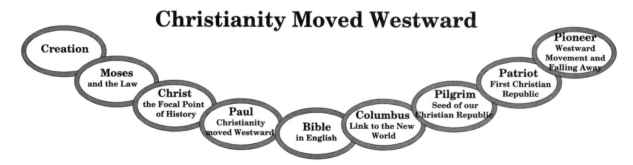

Each link is studied each year with the seed of the link being presented in kindergarten and expanded through the elementary grades. This allows the teacher to review the materials learned in the previous year(s) and build upon that foundation. By building the elementary history program upon expanding links the student will complete his elementary education with a great mastery of Christianity's effect upon the domestic, ecclesiastical, and civil sphere, i.e., the relationship between Christian liberty and external religious and civil liberty.

Christianity Moved Westward
Expanding the Links Through the Elementary School

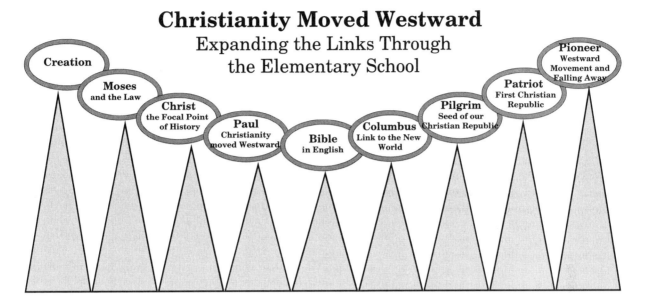

The question is often asked: how can the same link be taught each year without being repetitious? The goal is to expand each link through the elementary years with a diversity of ideas thereby teaching without repetition.

The following chart provides the overview of ideas which may be included each year in the elementary school. The ideas for *The Mighty Works of God: Self Government* were derived and expanded from the second year of the chart.

Kindergarten—Sixth Grade
Christianity Moved Westward

	CREATION	MOSES and the Law	CHRIST Focal Point of History	PAUL Westward Movement	BIBLE in English	CHRISTOPHER COLUMBUS Link to the New World	PILGRIM Seed of our Christian Republic	PATRIOT First Christian Republic	PIONEER Westward Movement & Falling Away
FIRST YEAR (Kindergarten)	God's Principle of Individuality — God as Creator — Christian Individuality	Moses Preserved By God — Infancy	Jesus: Birth and Reason for Coming	Story of Paul	John Wycliffe	Christopher Columbus	Thanksgiving Story	George Washington Father of our Country	Abraham Lincoln
SECOND YEAR (First Grade)	Man is God's Property •••••••••••••• Geographic Individuals	Moses Preserved by God for His purpose as First Historian and First Lawgiver — First 40 Years	Jesus Christ — The basis for Christian self government	Christianity moves Westward to Europe — Macedonian Call	John Wycliffe •••••••••••••• William Tyndale	Christopher Columbus	America's Heritage of Christian Character — Brotherly love & Christian care	George Washington Father of our Country	Abraham Lincoln
THIRD YEAR (Second Grade)	God's Character Revealed in Creation — Infinity, Diversity, Individuality	Moses Prepared to Lead Children of Israel from Captivity — Last 80 years — Principle of Representation. Deut. 1	Jesus coming changed history B.C.—A.D.	Paul's internal change — from persecutor to missionary	Geneva Bible	Providential Preparation of Columbus — Marco Polo's voyages	America's Heritage of Christian Character — Faith and Steadfastness — Diligence and Industry	Declaration of Independence — America declares herself an individual nation	Lewis and Clark

The Mighty Works of God: Self Government

	CREATION	MOSES and the Law	CHRIST Focal Point of History	PAUL Westward Movement	BIBLE in English	CHRISTOPHER COLUMBUS Link to the New World	PILGRIM Seed of our Christian Republic	PATRIOT First Christian Republic	PIONEER Westward Movement & Falling Away
FOURTH YEAR (Third Grade)	Origin & dispersion of the Races — Noah's 3 sons	Ten Commandments — Dual Form of Government	Christ came to fulfill the law Matt. 5:17-20	Paul on Mars Hill	King James Bible	Providence of God — Prince Henry and Navigational Instruments — America Preserved until He had a people ready	Providence of God — Bible — Holland — John Smith	God's Providence in American Revolution	Land of the Free
FIFTH YEAR (Fourth Grade)	Establishment of Civil Gov't. Gen. 9:6	Ten Commandments — God's law the basis of civil law	Law and the Gospel—the basis of our Government	Purpose of God's law as identified by Paul	Magna Charta — Individual rights protected by written law	Origin of the name America •••••••••••••••• Cabot's claim to North America	Voluntary Consent: Key to Self Government — Mayflower Compact	Samuel Adams — Christian Patriot	State History
SIXTH YEAR (Fifth Grade)	Christian Idea of Man and Gov't/ Pagan Idea of Man and Gov't	Hebrew Republic vs. Monarchy I Sam. 8	"In the fullness of time Christ came" — Greece & Rome prepared the soil for Christianity	Purpose of civil government as declared in Paul's writings	Bible — Basis of Reformation	Mexico and Canada claimed by Spain/France	Contrast Jamestown/ Plymouth	Patriotic Letters — Committees of Correspondence •••••••••••••••• Boston Patriots and Boston Tea Party	Herbert Hoover
SEVENTH YEAR (Sixth Grade)	Creation vs. Evolution	Distinctives of Moral law, Ritual law, Civil law	Two Systems of Law — Roman Civil Law — English Common Law — External/ Internal	New Testament Church —"a little Republic"	Bible and the Constitution	Contribution of Columbus to Westward Movement	Communism vs. Free Enterprise	Our Constitution: Law of the Land •••••••••••••••• Republic vs. Democracy — Prin. of Rep.; 3 branches of gov't; Dual Form of gov't	Ronald Reagan American Federalism

This overview has been developed with the intent of building line upon line, precept upon precept. The chart was originally published in *A Guide to American Christian Education for the Home and School.*

Part II

USING THE TEACHER'S GUIDE

Teacher Preparation

As the American Christian educator considers the teaching of any event or individual, the key is to determine the *Leading Ideas* to be presented to the students. The classroom content should be centered around the Idea to be taught, and supported by the facts and material selected for classroom use. The Ideas chosen must support the general Course Objectives. The following suggested general Course Objectives are reasoned from a Providential interpretation of history:

Course Objectives

1. To recognize the Providential Hand of God in all events, past, present, and future.

2. To recognize the importance of each individual in God's plan of history.

3. To teach the key links God used to move Christianity westward.

4. To teach the Biblical principles of government which formed the American Christian Constitutional Republic.

5. To learn to reason from cause to effect in historic events.

6. To recognize the stewardship responsibility of the American Christian for this nation.

Developing a General Course Overview

To direct the planning of the elementary history course, the teacher should prepare an overview for the year to determine the number of days or weeks to be spent on each of the nine links and its expansion. The length of time spent on each link will vary within the year, and from year to year. For example, one might spend one or two weeks on most links but six to eight weeks on just one.

Following is a suggested Course Overview based upon the Ideas identified in the Teacher's Guide. Each teacher must individualize his Overview to reflect the peculiar needs and background of the students being taught.

Suggested Course Overview

I. Introduction   2-3 weeks

    A. Why do we study history?
    B. Definitions—history, government, self government
    C. God's Hand of care—Providence
        1. Definition
        2. Biblical and historic examples
    D. Christianity moved westward

II. Creation   1-2 weeks

    A. In the beginning
    B. God created the continents
    C. God created man

III. Moses and the Law   1-2 weeks

    A. Moses preserved by God for His purpose as first historian
        and first lawgiver
    B. Moses as first historian

IV. Christ—the Focal Point of History   1 week

    A. Christ came to change the hearts of men.
    B. Christ made internal, Christian self government possible.

V. Paul and the Westward Movement of Christianity   1 week

    A. The Macedonian call
    B. Westward movement of Christianity to Europe

VI. Bible in English   2-3 weeks

    A. John Wycliffe, Morning Star of the Reformation
    B. The Printing Press
    C. William Tyndale, Father of the English Bible

VII. Christopher Columbus—Link to the New World   3-4 weeks

    A. God's Providence in opening the New World for exploration
    B. God prepared Columbus to lead in unknown paths

VIII. Pilgrim—Seed of our Christian Republic   3-5 weeks

    A. The Jamestown Colony prepared the way for the Pilgrims

B. God's Providence in the Pilgrim Story
C. "America's Heritage of Christian Character"—Brotherly love and Christian care

IX. Patriot - First Christian Republic   4-5 weeks

A. The world's first Christian Republic established upon Biblical principles of self and civil government
B. George Washington, Father of Our Country
C. Men of character and courage expanded the republic on the frontier—Daniel Boone.

X. Pioneer - Westward Movement   6-8 weeks

A. The obstacles to maintaining a nation of unity with diversity required Biblical character and reasoning.
B. Communication united the nation and advanced inventions and industry.
C. Diversity with unity is demonstrated in the individuality and sovereignty of each state.

XI. Conclusion   1/2-1 week

Expanding the Course Overview

After the teacher has determined the general topics to be covered during the year, i.e., the General Course Overview, he should expand the Overview to include the specific ideas to be covered with the students.

The Expanded Course Overview will identify the Leading Ideas for each general topic and the number of days for teaching each idea. Beginning on page 15 of the Teacher's Guide, suggested Leading Ideas have been included for each chapter of the Student Text. The teacher may select from the suggested Leading Ideas or include additional Ideas of his own choosing.

The following Expanded Course Overview is for the Introduction to the course.

Expanded Course Overview

I. Introduction   2-3 Weeks

A. **His Story** — *Chapter 1*   2-3 Days

1. History is His Story
2. Studying History will help us to recognize God's

Hand as He works in the lives of men and
nations
3. God commands us to remember all He has done
for us as individuals and nations

B. **Government** — *Chapter 2*   3-4 Days

1. Government is direction and control
2. Internal is causative to the external
3. If I govern myself well, I will not need others
to control me

C. **Civil Government** — *Chapter 3*   2-3 Days

1. God has a plan for civil government
2. The individual is responsible for civil government

D. **God's Providence** — *Chapter 4*   4-5 Days

1. God cares for His creatures
2. God cares for men in a special way, for "Ye
are of more value . . ."
3. God's care and protection are seen in History
a. Feeding of the five thousand
b. The Pilgrims find a new home and a friend

E. **Christianity Moved Westward**   1-2 Days

1. God used individual men and nations to move the
Gospel westward

Developing Lesson Plans

Part III of the Teacher's Guide is designed to assist the teacher in developing lesson plans for daily instruction. The Idea to be comprehended by the student must be clearly identified by the teacher and must govern the content of the class-time and any student work. Suggested Leading Ideas have been given for each chapter of the Student Text. The teacher may select from these Ideas, or add additional Ideas.

Several essentials should be included

in the lesson plan: summary statement of the Leading Idea to be covered, reading, discussion, notes, and student written work.

Teachers might find it beneficial to prepare lesson plans for a complete section of their expanded overview at one time. When beginning the lesson plans for each section of the overview, the teacher could write the Leading Idea for each day into the lesson plan before including the specific information necessary for the class. Planning for one or two weeks at a time helps insure that the teacher will cover the amount of material necessary during that time and also allows for a continuous train of thought rather than individual, isolated lessons.

To provide a classroom which will produce a love of learning in the student, a variety of approaches to the daily class-time should be included in the plans—consideration must always be given to the age and capacity of the students. Primary age students may read the book aloud together during the classtime, reason concerning the main ideas, record simple notes, answer written questions, outline maps, and color pictures. Students of all ages enjoy special projects and events which enhance the material and bring it to life. Part III of the Teacher's Guide identifies many suggestions to aid in developing the student's ability to reflect and reason concerning historic events.

As stated previously, a key ingredient in preparing lessons is variety; the teacher should attempt to incorporate into the lesson plans different teaching methodologies, including various types of discussion, notes, and student work.

Suggestions for *Supplemental Activities* have been included. These activities provide opportunities for additional study, special celebrations, or field trips, which will enhance the course of study.

Student Recording

By the first grade, the main Ideas to be remembered by the student should become a part of their permanent record in the notebook, with adequate facts to support the Idea. This recording may be accomplished in a variety of ways:

A sentence(s) which reflects the Leading Idea may be recorded. Charts showing contrasts, comparisons, cause to effect, or effect to cause are effective in developing reasoning skills. Timelines demonstrate the Providence of God in events of history. The student may simply record a list which reflects the fruit of reasoning from the Leading Idea.

Outlines may be utilized by the teacher, but should be limited to one day or unit of teaching, keeping the teacher and student from becoming encumbered by the tedium of the outline.

For the primary age student, the charts, timelines, or outlines are kept simple in their form and content.

A variety of *Suggested Student Notes* have been included in Part III of the Teacher's Guide.

Student Written Work

The confirmation of the Idea being taught will occur as the student has the opportunity to reflect and reason concerning the Idea taught. Suggestions for student written work are included in Part III of the Teacher's Guide, in the section *Cultivating Student Mastery*.

Student Activity Pages are included on the CD with the Teacher's Guide. These pages provide many opportunities for the student to reason with the Ideas presented in the Student Text.

The student work should be devised to demand reasoning from the Leading Idea being considered, not just the recording of facts. These exercises must be evaluated as to their appropriateness for the capacity of the students and the preparation given during the classtime.

Drawing or coloring pictures illustrating the events studied will be enjoyed by students of all ages. Original art may be checked as to its accuracy in representation of the event.

Maps provide an excellent opportunity for the student to produce a geographical essay which confirms his comprehension of the Idea covered.

Questions which involve short answers may be given. Consider that questions asking who, what, when, and where are fact-centered and identify the student's comprehension, but do not require reasoning. Questions addressing why, considering cause to effect or effect to cause, or expecting the student to draw conclusions demand that the student exercise reasoning. The teacher should keep in mind that questions which demand reasoning will require more time in answering than simply reproducing facts which have been presented.

Short essays may be written by the primary student; a first grade student should be able to write a simple essay by the second semester. Essays should be specifically related to the Idea which the teacher has presented in the classroom.

By second semester of first grade, simple guided research may be performed by the student. For the primary student, the teacher would probably find it best to have available in the classroom the resources which are appropriate for the grade level, and provide questions which would guide the student in his research.

Map Instructions

Preparation of maps will confirm the geographic setting of historic events in the student's mind. Historian Katherine Dang identified instructions for map work in *A Guide to American Christian Education for the Home and School.* The following simplified instructions have been derived from that work.

1. Map work is mainly outlining and let-

tering. There is no filling-in of areas with solid coloring.

2. Rivers, shorelines of lakes, coastlines of seas and oceans are outlined with blue. Rivers are outlined along *one side* of the drawn line.

3. Outlining will follow along the exact course of the printed lines.

4. Labeling is to be straight and even on the map. Drawing two lines with a ruler will provide control of the size of letter.

5. All labeling is in manuscript. The size of letters may vary, i.e. names of countries will be larger than names of cities.[5]

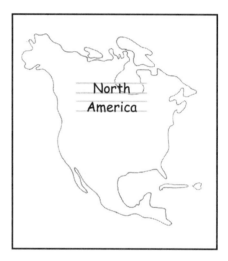

Sample Lesson Plans

Following are sample lesson plans for teaching the Leading Ideas for the first two chapters of the Student Text. They are intended for a primary level classroom, with a classtime of approximately twenty to twenty-five minutes.

Sample Lesson Plan

His Story

Leading Idea: History is His Story

Read: Page 1 of Student Text

Reflection and Reasoning:
- How do we measure time? Consider that there was no time before God created the heavens and the earth. God has lived forever.
- Review the ways that time is identified — the clock and calendar.
- When did time begin?
- Identify the evidence of the Bible being a book of history.
- Why do we say that history is "His Story?"

Student Activity:
- Sing familiar songs which identify God's character. Or, begin to teach a new song. Examples: *I Sing the Mighty Power of God; And God Said; All Things Bright and Beautiful; Psalm 78.*

Student Notes:
    History is His Story.

Cultivating Student Mastery
    1. What is history?

Sample Lesson Plan

His Story

Leading Idea: Studying History will help us to recognize God's Hand as He works in the lives of men and nations.

Introducing the lesson:
- Review the definition of history.
- Review the idea that time begins with creation.

Reflection and Reasoning:
- Do you have a record of the history of your family? Picture albums of past generations? Can you see how God gave you each person in your family and how they each made a special contribution? History is a record of the people of the earth and shows how God has worked in the lives of individuals, families, cities, states, and nations.
- Look at family histories or picture albums that show several generations of a family. These illustrate the idea of a family's history.
- How would looking at a history of our family help us to see how God has worked in our family?

Sample Lesson Plan

His Story

Leading Idea: God commands us to remember all He has done for us as individuals and nations.

Introducing the lesson:
- Review the definition of history.
- What does it mean to *remember*?

Read: Page 2 of Student Text.

Reflection and Reasoning:
- How does looking at a family history or picture album help us to remember the history of our family? What would happen if we never looked at a family history or at a picture album or framed pictures?
- What types of things do we *remember*, or never forget? Our names, our birthdays? What types of things must our parents *remember*? God wants us to *remember* what He has done in our lives and in our nation.
- How will studying history help us to *remember* what God has done? If we *remember* what God has done, would it help us to love God more? Why or why not?

Student Activity:
- Read selected Bible verses about *remembering*: Deuteronomy 7:18; 8:2.
- Identify a list of things we want to remember about ourselves, our family, and our country.

Student Notes:
We study History to remember what God has done.

Cultivating Student Mastery:
1. How does remembering History help us love God more?

Sample Lesson Plan

Government

Leading Idea: Government is direction and control.

Introducing the lesson:
- Review: What is history? Why should we study history?

Read: Page 3 of Student Text.

Reflection and Reasoning:
- What is government? Webster's definition in the 1828 *Dictionary* is "direction" and "control".
- What is direction? Have you seen a policeman at the corner? What is he doing? He is giving direction to those who are driving down the street.
- When mother or father or teacher tells us how to complete a task, that is direction.

- If we do not follow the direction of the policeman, what will happen? What happens if we do not follow our parent's or teacher's directions?
- What is control? When you ride your bicycle, what determines how fast it is going? Who is controlling the speed? When *you* decide what to wear, who is controlling? When you decide what you say, who is controlling? When you decide what to eat, who is controlling?
- We must conclude that there are two spheres or ways in which we are governed — internal and external. If we do not govern our own actions internally, we will be governed externally.
- When we are at home, we will be governed (directed and controlled) by our parents. When we are at school, we will be governed by our teachers. In the nation, we are governed by civil government.

Student Activity:
- Use *Student Activity Page 2-1*. Label the chart with the two spheres of government: Internal and External.

Student Notes:
  Government is direction and control?

Cultivating Student Mastery:
  1. What is government?

Sample Lesson Plan

Government

Leading Idea: Internal is causative to the external.

Introducing the lesson:
- Review: What is government?

Read: Pages 3-4 of Student Text.

Reflection and Reasoning:
- How do you decide what you are going to say? How do you decide what you are going to wear? How do you decide what you are going to eat or what you are going to do? The ideas or thoughts in the heart cause us to decide each of these areas.
- If our thoughts and ideas are controlled by the Bible, then what we say or do will be governed by the Bible. The Bible confirms this truth in Matthew 12:35.
- Develop a chart on the board which identifies the cause and effect relationship seen in Matthew 12:35. If I have good treasure in my heart, what kinds of things will I do? If I have evil things in my heart, what kinds of things will I do? See Teacher's Guide, p. 23.

Student Activity:
- Use *Student Activity Page 2-2*. Record the basic chart for Matthew 12:35.

Cultivating Student Mastery:
1. Why are the thought and ideas we have in our heart and mind important?

Sample Lesson Plan

Government

Leading Idea: If I govern myself well, I will not need others to control me.

Read: Pages 4-6 of Student Text.

Reflection and Reasoning:
• Consider the questions stated by Louisa May Alcott in her poem: How can I learn to rule myself? How can I be the child I should? How can I keep a sunny soul? How can I tune my little heart to sweetly sing all day?
• How can we learn what God wants us to do? How can we be controlled by the Word of God? Why should we listen to our parents, teachers, and the preacher in our church?
• Will we be happier if we govern the kingdom of our own hearts or if we must be controlled by someone else? Why?

Student Activity:
• Read Psalm 119:11 in the Bible.
• Prepare craft of Psalm 119:11. *Student Activity Pages 2-3* and *2-4.*
• Sing *Thy Word have I Hid in My Heart.*

Part III

INTRODUCTION
Chapters 1-4
2-3 Weeks

Each year the history course should begin with the basic concepts which are the premise for reasoning throughout the entire study. These basic truths reflect the philosophy of history on which the course is built.

The rudiments of the history course must be introduced, even to the youngest student. These elements are simplified or deepened according to the age of the child.

Chapters 1-4 of the Student Text contain the introductory philosophy of history and the major premises to guide the student's reasoning.

Caution: Do not oversimplify. The young child can understand such words as history, government, and Providence.

Leading Ideas

When presenting each day's lesson, the teacher should have specific goals. The main goal should be to teach a Leading Idea through the reading, facts, discussion, and other class activities. *This leading idea is a conclusion to which the teacher should reason with the students.*

Suggested Leading Ideas are highlighted in boxes. Pages from the Student Text are identified below the Leading Idea. Some Ideas may be taught with no reading in the Student Text.

Explanatory material, for the teacher, follows each leading idea.

Chapter 1
His Story
2-3 Days

Leading Ideas

History is His Story.

Student Text, page 1

Note: Explanatory or resource material, for the teacher's study, follows most of the suggested Leading Ideas.

• Noah Webster's 1828 *Dictionary* defines history: "An account of facts, particularly of facts respecting nations or states; a narration of events in the order in which they happened, with their cause and effect." The last phrase of this definition — with their cause and effect — distinguishes a Providential view of history.

• Rev. S. W. Foljambe preached a sermon in 1876 — *The Hand of God in American History.* He included this declaration of history: "It has been said that history is the biography of communities; in another, and profounder sense, it is the autobiography of him 'who worketh all things after the counsel of his own will' (Eph. 1:11), and who is graciously timing all events in the interests of his Christ, and of the kingdom of God on earth."[6]

• God is eternal and infinite. He has no beginning or ending. History, therefore, begins when God created the heavens and the earth, as recorded in Genesis 1.

• Time begins only with the creation of the earth.

• The Scriptures reveal the fact that God not only created heaven and earth, but has been working in the lives of men and nations since the beginning of time. Therefore, History is His Story or God's Story. It is the record of God working in the lives of men and nations.

For Reflection and Reasoning

Note: Numerous suggestions have been given for discussion and activities. The teacher must select from these suggestions, considering the age and capacity of the students.

• How do we measure time? Consider

that there was no time before God created the heavens and the earth. God has lived forever.

• Identify the evidence of the Bible being a book of history.

• Why do we say that history is "His Story"?

• Review the ways that time is identified — the clock and calendar.

• Sing familiar songs which identify God's character. Or, begin to teach a new song. Examples: *I Sing the Mighty Power of God; And God Said; All Things Bright and Beautiful; Psalm 78.*

Suggested Student Notes

History is His Story.

Reminder: Student Notes must be kept to an appropriate length for the age of the child. A first grade student might record only the equivalent of one sentence in one day. A second grade student might record only the equivalent of two sentences in one day, etc.

Cultivating Student Mastery

Have the students answer the following question (oral or written):

1. What is history?

Leading Idea

Studying History will help us to recognize God's Hand as He works in the lives of men and nations.

• Rev. Foljambe, in 1876, cautioned Americans against a failure to study Providential history: "The more thoroughly a nation deals with its history, the more decidedly will it recognize and own an overruling Providence therein, and the more religious a nation will it become; while the more superficially it deals with its history, seeing only secondary causes and human agencies, the more irreligious will it be."[7]

• Consider: Why is the study of Providential History important to the American Christian? How would understanding Providential History aid the individual in understanding that God has a unique purpose for each individual?

For Reflection and Reasoning

• Do you have a record of the history of your family? Picture albums of past generations? Can you see how God gave you each person in your family and how they each made a special contribution? History is a record of the people of the earth and shows how God has worked in the lives of individuals, families, cities, states, and nations.

• Look at family histories or picture albums that show several generations of a family. These illustrate the idea of a family's history.

Leading Idea

God commands us to remember all He has done for us as individuals and nations.

Student Text, page 2

• Noah Webster states that "to remember is to have in the mind an idea which had been in the mind before, and which recurs to the mind without effort."

• Consider the many Scriptures that deal with the command for remembering what God has done. Examples: Deuteronomy 7:18; 8:2; Psalm 78:1-11.

For Reflection and Reasoning

• How does looking at a family history or picture album help us to remember the history of our family? What would happen if we never looked at a family history, a picture album, or framed pictures?

• What types of things do we *remember*, or never forget? Our names, our birthdays? What types of things must our parents *remember*? God wants us to *remember* what He has done in our lives and what He has done in our nation. Read selected verses on remembering.

• Identify a list of things we want to remember about ourselves, our family, and our country.

Suggested Student Notes

We study History to remember what God has done.

Cultivating Student Mastery

1. How does remembering History help us love God more?

Chapter 2
Government

3-4 Days

Leading Idea

Government is direction and control.

Student Text, page 3

• When the typical American of today thinks of government, he thinks first of civil government. But the Christian realizes that he should be directed and controlled internally, by the Word of God.

• Government, therefore, has two spheres — internal and external. Each individual will be directed or controlled, either by that which is within (internal) or that which is without (external).

For Reflection and Reasoning

• Review: What is history? Why should we study history?

• What is government? Webster's definition in the 1828 *Dictionary* is "direction" and "control."

• What is direction? Have you seen a policeman at the corner? What is he doing? He is giving direction to those who are driving down the street.
   When mother or father or teacher tells us how to complete a task, that is direction.

• If we do not follow the direction of the policeman, what will happen? What happens if we do not follow our parent's or teacher's directions?

• What is control? When you ride your bicycle, what determines how fast it is going? Who is controlling the speed? When *you* decide what to wear, who is controlling? When *you* decide what you say, who is controlling? When *you* decide what to eat, who is controlling?

• We must conclude that there are two spheres or ways in which we are governed — internal and external. If we do not govern our own actions internally, we will be governed externally.

• When we are at home, we will be governed (directed and controlled) by our parents. When we are at school, we will be governed by our teachers. In the nation, we are governed by civil government.

• Label a chart which identifies the two spheres of government — internal and external. See *Student Activity Page 2-1.* This chart could be titled "Government." Label the two spheres of government as

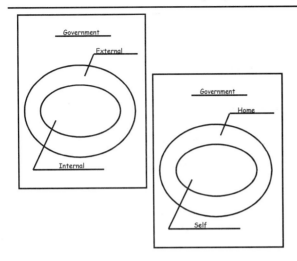

"Internal" and "External." Or "Self" and "Home." Or "Home" and "School," "Church," or "Civil." Choose appropriate labels based upon the class discussion.

Suggested Student Notes

Government is direction and control.

Cultivating Student Mastery

1. What is government?

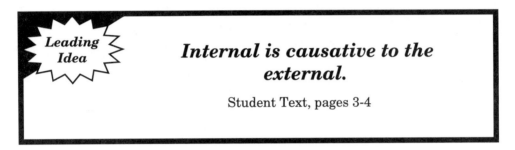

> **Leading Idea**
>
> ## *Internal is causative to the external.*
>
> Student Text, pages 3-4

• There are two spheres of government: internal and external.

• Proverbs 23:7a teaches: "For as a man thinketh in his heart, so is he." Proverbs 4:23 tells: "Keep thy heart with all diligence for out of it are the issues of life." These verses teach us that the heart will direct and control one's actions.

• Matthew 12:35 confirms the idea of the internal sphere being causative to the external sphere.

• Many Scriptures reveal that the first century Christians demonstrated they had the *law of God* written on their hearts and controlling their actions. See Romans 2:15; II Corinthians 3:3; Hebrews 8:10; 10:16.

For Reflection and Reasoning

• Review: How do you decide what you are going to say? How do you decide what you are going to wear? How do you decide what you are going to eat or what you are going to do? The ideas or thoughts in the heart cause us to decide each of these areas.

• If our thoughts and ideas are controlled by the Bible, then what we say or do will be governed by the Bible. The Bible confirms this truth in Matthew 12:35.

• On the board, identify the cause and effect relationship in Matthew 12:35. Consider how the internal is causative to the external. The teacher may choose to have the students record the basic chart for Student Notes. See *Student Activity Page 2-2.*

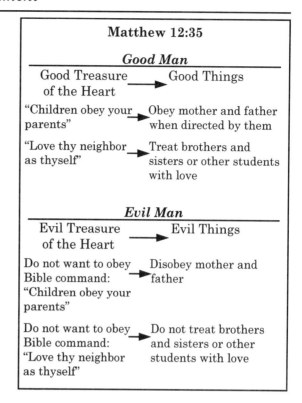

• Expand the chart developed from Matthew 12:35 with practical examples of "Good Treasure" and the effect in "Good Things." Also illustrate "Evil Treasure" and "Evil Things." This chart may be developed and expanded as the teacher desires. Consider specific rules or laws which govern the home or classroom and the effect of those who have "Good Treasure" in their hearts as contrasted to those who have "Evil Treasure." *The expanded chart would not be recorded in the student's notebook.*

Cultivating Student Mastery

1. Why are the thoughts and ideas we have in our heart and mind important?

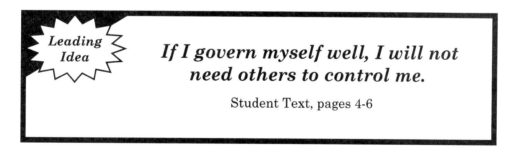

If I govern myself well, I will not need others to control me.

Student Text, pages 4-6

• Proverbs 16:32 instructs: "He that is slow to anger is better than the mighty; and he that ruleth his spirit than he that taketh a city." The comparison of controlling one's anger and spirit to "he that taketh a city" implies the difficult task of governing oneself.

"He that gets and keeps the mastery of his passions *is better than the mighty, better than he that* by a long siege *takes a city* or by a long war subdues a country. Behold, a greater than Alexander or Caesar is here. The conquest of our-selves, and our own unruly passions, requires more true wisdom, and a more steady, constant, and regular management, than the obtaining of a victory over the forces of an enemy. A rational conquest is more honourable to a rational creature than a brutal one. It is a victory that does nobody any harm; no lives or treasures are sacrificed to it, but only some base lusts. It is harder, and therefore more glorious, to quash an insurrection at home than to resist an invasion from abroad; nay, such are the

gains of meekness that by it *we are more than conquerors.*"

Matthew Henry *Commentary*

• Only as we lean upon the Lord, trust in Him to guide our daily actions, and internalize His principles from the Word of God can we hope to govern our own actions.

For Reflection and Reasoning

• In her poem, *My Kingdom,* Louisa May Alcott states the conflict of governing well the internal thoughts of the mind. Consider her questions and answers: *How can I learn to rule myself? How can I be the child I should? How can I keep a sunny soul? How can I tune my little heart to sweetly sing all day?*

• How can we learn what God wants us to do? How can we be controlled by the Word of God? Why should we listen to our parents, teachers, and the preacher in our church?

• Will we be happier if we govern the kingdom of our own hearts or if we must be controlled by someone else? Why?

• Prepare craft of Psalm 119:11. See *Student Activity Pages 2-3* and *2-4.* Label top line — My Kingdom; Lines on each side of the heart can be labeled — thoughts and feelings. Cut opening on

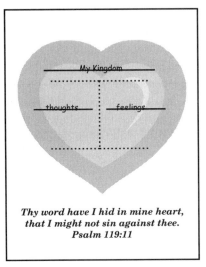

Thy word have I hid in mine heart, that I might not sin against thee.
Psalm 119:11

heart using dotted lines. Cut out Bible and glue Bible to back of page. When two sides are opened, the Bible will appear.

• Commit Psalm 119:11 to memory.

• Sing *Thy Word have I Hid in My Heart.*

24

Chapter 3
Civil Government
2-3 Days

Leading Idea

God has a plan for civil government.

Student Text, page 7

● The Christian idea of civil government deduced from the Scriptures is that all power comes from God to the individual. That power can then be delegated by the individual to each sphere of his life, including civil government. Civil government is given the power by the people to govern the city, state, or nation. I Peter 2:13-14; Romans 13:1-4.

For Reflection and Reasoning

● Review the definition of government.

● Civil government has the authority to make laws which will govern the people of that city, state, or nation.

The Bible teaches us that we are to obey the laws that are made in our land. The Bible also teaches us that those laws should be made according to the Bible.

How can rulers be sure to make good laws?

● In what city does your family live? In what state? In what nation? There are many families who live in the city. There are many more families who live in the state. And many, many families live in the nation.

● Look at a map of the city in which you live and consider the many families that live in a city.

Look at a map of the state in which you live and consider the many families that live in a state.

Look at a map of the United States and consider how many, many families live in the United States, and how important it is to have laws which protect the property of each individual and each family.

● Each family has his own property — house, furniture, clothing, dishes, toys, etc.

Since men are sinners, they might take some other person's property. Someone might try to keep families from obeying God, i.e. going to church, taking care of their own family, etc.

God planned for civil government to protect each individual and his family's liberty and property.

● When we study history, we find that there have been different kinds of civil government, some have been good and some have been bad. Do you remember that when Moses was born, the Egyptian

Pharaoh had the power to kill the baby boys? No one could stop him. We find that there were times in history when people were not allowed to go to the church which they wanted to attend.

God gave us our nation, the United States of America. In this nation, we have great liberty. We can choose what church to attend. Our personal property is protected.

Suggested Student Notes

Civil government controls and directs men in cities and nations.

Leading Idea

The individual is responsible for civil government.

Student Text, page 8

● There must always be *government*. The size and authority given to *civil government* will be in direct proportion to the extent of self government being exercised by the individuals, i.e. as the individual is more self governed, the size and authority of civil government will be lessened. If the individual is not self governed, the size and authority of civil government will be expanded.

For Reflection and Reasoning

● Review: What is government? What is self government? What is civil government?

Review the idea of *Internal is causative to the external.* How do we control our actions? See *Student Activity Page 2-1*.

● We must always be controlled. If we are not controlled internally, then we will have to be controlled externally. At home, if you are controlling your own thoughts and ideas according to the Bible, do you need the rules of your home? As families control themselves according to the Bible, do they need control from civil government?

If we do not control ourselves, will we need the rules in our home? What if families do not control themselves, will they need civil government to control them?

● Draw charts on the board to illustrate how the amount of government can be divided between the internal and external. If there is a large amount of self government, there will be a smaller amount of civil government. If there is a small amount of self government, there will be a large amount of civil government. If time permits, the charts could first relate to the idea of the balance between self and home or family government. This idea could then be extended and illustrated for family and civil government.

Who needs civil government the most? Who needs civil government the least?

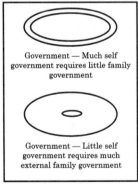

Government — Much self government requires little family government

Government — Little self government requires much external family government

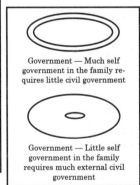

Government — Much self government in the family requires little civil government

Government — Little self government in the family requires much external civil government

Chapter 4
God's Providence
4-5 Days

> **Leading Idea**
>
> ## *God cares for His creatures.*
>
> Student Text, page 9

• Providence is defined by Webster as "timely care" or "providing or preparing for the future". Webster states further that Providence is "the care and superintendence which God exercises over his creatures. He that acknowledges a creation and denies a *providence,* involves himself in a palpable contradiction; for the same power which caused a thing to exist is necessary to continue its existence."

• Care is defined by Webster as "a looking to; regard; attention, or heed, with a view to safety or protection."

For Reflection and Reasoning

• Do you or a friend have a pet? Do you "care" for them? What is care?

• God cares for all of His creation — the fish of the sea, the birds in the air, the animals, even the plants.

• The Bible teaches about God's care for animals. Students may read the following verses and discern God's Providence in caring for His creatures:

Job 38:41 tells us that God cares for the ravens.

Psalm 147:9 tells us that God gives the beast his food.

Matthew 6:26 teaches us that God feeds the birds.

• Draw a picture of a bird or animal finding food God has prepared for it.

Suggested Student Notes

Providence is God's care for His creatures.

Leading Idea

God cares for men in a special way, for "Ye are of more value . . ."

Student Text, pages 9-10

• *"But the very hairs of your head are numbered.* Matthew 10:30. This is a proverbial expression, denoting the account which God takes and keeps of all the concernments of his people, even of those that are most minute, and least regarded. This is not to be made a matter of curious enquiry, but of encouragement to live in a continual dependence upon God's providential care, which extends itself to all occurrences, yet without disparagement to the infinite glory, or disturbance to the infinite rest, of the Eternal Mind. If God numbers their hairs, much more does he number their heads, and take care of their lives, their comforts, their souls. It intimates, that God takes more care of them, than they do of themselves. They who are solicitous to number their money, and goods, and cattle, yet were never careful to number their hairs, which fall and are lost, and they never miss them: but God *numbers the hairs of* his people, and *not a hair of their head shall perish* (Luke xxi. 18); not the least hurt shall be done them, but upon a valuable consideration: so precious to God are his saints, and their lives and deaths!"

Matthew Henry *Commentary*

For Reflection and Reasoning

• Review: How does God care for plants? How does God care for animals?

• How do your parents care for you? Do they make sure you have food? clothes? If you are sick, do they take care of you?

Our parents care for us very much, but God cares for us even more. God cares more about us than He does for the animals. God cares so much that he knows everything that happens to us. He knows when we are sad. He knows when we are afraid. He knows when we are happy. He knows when we obey Him or disobey Him. He knows even how many hairs are on our heads. Do you know how many hairs you have on your head? God cares a great deal for us, doesn't He?

How does God show His care for children?

• See *Student Activity Page 4-1*. The student may glue his picture on the page, reminding him that God cares for him. Student notes may be recorded on activity page.

• Sing songs dealing with God's Providence: *Oh, Be Careful; God is So Good; I Will Sing of the Mercies of the Lord; His Eye is on the Sparrow.*

Suggested Student Notes

Each man, woman, boy, and girl is important to God.

Cultivating Student Mastery

1. What is God's Providence?

Leading Idea

God's care and protection are seen in History.

Student Text, pages 10-11

Feeding of the Five Thousand

• ". . . Christ could have fed them by miracle, but to set us an example of providing for those of our own household, he will have their own camp victualled in an ordinary way. Here is neither plenty, nor variety, nor dainty; a dish of fish was no rarity to them that were fishermen, but it was food convenient for the twelve; two fishes for their supper, and bread to serve them perhaps for a day or two: here was no wine or strong drink; fair water from the rivers in the desert was the best they had to drink with their meat; and yet out of this Christ will have the multitude fed. . .

"Though the disproportion was so great, yet there was enough and to spare. . .

"It is the same divine power, though exerted in an ordinary way, which multiplies *the seed sown in the ground* every year, and makes *the earth yield her increase;* so that was brought out by handfuls, is brought home in sheaves. *This is the Lord's doing;* it is *by Christ* that all natural things consist, and *by the word of his power* that they are upheld."

Matthew Henry *Commentary*

For Reflection and Reasoning

• Review: What is Providence?

• Consider that the Bible tells us that there were 5,000 men, plus women and children. There probably were over 10,000 people fed from the five loaves and two fishes.

• How does the story of the *Feeding of the Five Thousand* remind us of God's care for His people? How was God's power revealed in this event?

• Sing songs that identify God's power: *I Sing the Mighty Power of God; My God is So Big.*

• Draw or color a picture of Jesus feeding the five thousand with the loaves and fishes.

Suggested Student Notes

God's Providence is seen in history.

Leading Idea

God's care and protection are seen in History.

Student Text, pages 11-12

The Pilgrims Find a New Home and a Friend

• Many Americans are familiar with Squanto's assistance to the Pilgrims. Reasoning Providentially, the American Christian must recognize God's Hand in bringing the Pilgrims to Cape Cod, where a place was prepared for their settlement and Squanto was waiting.

• William Bradford recorded the details of the Pilgrim's settlement of Plymouth in his history, *Of Plimouth Plantation.*

Setting out for the New World, with a patent for the northern parts of Virginia, God saw fit to guide their ship to the shores of Cape Cod, landing far north of their planned destination.

• God, in His wisdom, had made special preparation for this small band of settlers. One of the special preparations was to have the Indian Squanto there to be a friend to them. What a surprise it was to the Pilgrims to have an Indian who spoke their language. Only an all-wise God could arrange for their ship to land at this particular location.

For Reflection and Reasoning

• Review: What is Providence?

• Review the landing of the Pilgrims at Cape Cod. What special events reveal that their arrival in Cape Cod was specially planned by God?

• Consider that the winds and waves are guided by God. Although this group of settlers had planned to arrive in Virginia, God guided their ship to Cape Cod.

Later this year, in our study of history, we will learn even more of why it was important for the Pilgrims to arrive in Cape Cod.

• Many times we make plans for what we think is best, but God has something better for us.

• Look at a map of North America. See how far off course the Mayflower was when it arrived at Cape Cod rather than Virginia.

• On the board, make a list of specific events which occurred, revealing God's Providence in the arrival of the Pilgrims at Cape Cod:
  • Ship guided by God
  • Squanto knew English
  • Squanto helped them

See *Student Activity Page 4-2.* All or selected items from the list may be recorded by the students.

Christianity Moved Westward
1-2 Days

> **Leading Idea**
>
> *God used individual men and nations to move the Gospel westward.*

• History records the evidence of God's use of individual men and nations to move Christianity westward with its effect in the civil sphere. This westward movement produced America and her Christian form of government.

Historian Verna Hall identified individuals, events, and nations, used of God, to bring forth America and her form of government. See *The Christian History of the Constitution,* page 6A.

• *The Mighty Works of God: Self Government* identifies key links used by God to move Christianity westward. See pages 2 and 3 for the links to be included in this year's study.

For Reflection and Reasoning

• Review: What is History? What is Providence?

• Our study of history this year — *The Mighty Works of God: Self Government* — will be looking at individuals God used to give us our nation, the United States of America. Each individual is important, like the links on a chain.

• When Christ came to the earth, He lived on the continent of Asia. Christianity was first on the continent of Asia. The Gospel was taken from Asia to Europe, and from Europe to North America. The Gospel was the basis of the ideas found in our nation's constitution.

• Locate the continents of Asia, Europe, and North America on a map. Emphasize how the Gospel moved from continent to continent.

• Look at a chain and discuss the importance of each link. Relate that God has used individuals to move the Gospel westward to produce our nation. Each one is important in His Story.

• Use *Student Activity Pages 4-3* and *4-4* to briefly introduce the students to the key links to be studied this year in the history class. Cut and glue the pictures for the links of Creation, Moses, Paul, Columbus, and the Pioneer Link.

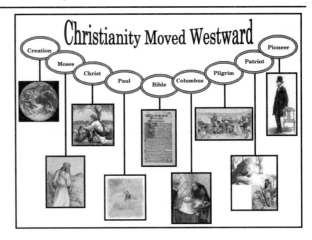

Supplemental Activities

• Begin a simple history of your school, with pictures, dates, etc.

• If possible, visit a county or state capitol. Students could see the elected officials who make and enforce the laws.

If you do not live near a seat of civil government, pictures could be found of such locations, and discussed with the student.

CREATION

Chapters 5-7
1-2 Weeks

Chapter 5
In the Beginning

2-3 Days

> **Leading Idea**
>
> ***In the beginning God created the heaven and the earth. Genesis 1:1***
>
> Student Text, page 13

• Noah Webster defined *create:* "To produce; to bring into being from nothing; to cause to exist." Only God can create.

• The Scriptures confirm the creation of the earth. See John 1:3, Colossians 1:16, and many others.

• "(3.) The manner in which this work was effected: *God created it,* that is, made it out of nothing. There was not any pre-existent matter out of which the world was produced. The fish and fowl were indeed produced out of the waters and the beasts and man out of the earth; but that earth and those waters were made out of nothing. By the ordinary power of nature, it is impossible that any things should be made out of nothing; no artificer can work, unless he has something to work on. But by the almighty power of God it is not only possible that something should be made of nothing (the God of nature is not subject to the laws of nature), but in the creation it is impossible it should be otherwise, for nothing is more injurious to the honour of the Eternal Mind than the supposition of eternal matter. Thus the excellency of the power is of God and all the glory is to him.

"(4.) When this work was produced: *In the beginning,* that is, in the beginning of time, when that clock was first set a going: time began with the production of those beings that are measured by time. Before the beginning of time there was none but that Infinite Being that inhabits eternity. Should we ask why God made the world no sooner, we should but darken counsel by words without knowledge; for how could there be sooner or later in eternity? And he did make it in the beginning of time, ac- cording to his eternal counsels before all time. . ."

Matthew Henry *Commentary*

For Reflection and Reasoning

• Review: What is history? When does it begin? When does time begin?

• What did God use to create the heaven and the earth?

• Can we "create" from nothing?

• Read selected verses from Genesis 1.

• Using the selected verses, review each of the Days of Creation. See *Student Activity Pages 5-1* and *5-2*. Students cut and glue appropriate picture to identify each day of creation.

• Sing songs which teach of God's character, creation, or specifically the power of God. Examples: *I Sing the Mighty Power of God; And God Said; All Things Bright and Beautiful; This is My Father's World.*

In the beginning God created the heaven and the earth.
Genesis 1:1

Create is to make from nothing.

• Use *Student Activity Page 5-3* to confirm the idea that God *created* the heaven and the earth. Record Student Notes on this page.

Suggested Student Notes

Create is to make from nothing.

Leading Idea

Creation reveals God's character.

Student Text, pages 13-16

• The record of creation teaches us many things about God. "Observe, in this verse, four things: — (1.) The effect produced—*the heaven and the earth,* that is, the world, including the whole frame and furniture of the universe, the *world and all things therein,* Acts xvii. 24. The world is a great house, consisting of upper and lower stories, the structure stately and magnificent, uniform and convenient, and every room well and wisely furnished. It is the visible part of the creation that Moses here designs to account for; therefore he mentions not the creation of angels. But as the earth has not only its surface adorned with grass and flowers, but also its bowels enriched with metals and precious stones (which partake more of its solid nature and are more valuable, though the creation of them is not mentioned here), so the heavens are not only beautified to our eye with glorious lamps which garnish its outside, of whose creation we here read, but they are within replenished with glorious beings, out of our

34

sight, more celestial, and more surpassing them in worth and excellency than the gold or sapphires surpass the lilies of the field. In the visible world it is easy to observe, [1.] Great variety, several sorts of beings vastly differing in their nature and constitution from each other. *Lord, how manifold are thy works,* and all good! [2.] Great beauty. The azure sky and verdant earth are charming to the eye of the curious spectator, much more the ornaments of both. How transcendent then must the beauty of the Creator be! [3.] Great exactness and accuracy. To those that, with the help of microscopes, narrowly look into the works of nature, they appear far more fine than any of the works of art. [4.] Great power. It is not a lump of dead and inactive matter, but there is virtue, more or less, in every creature: the earth itself has a magnetic power. [5.] Great order, a mutual dependence of beings, an exact harmony of motions, and an admirable chain and connection of causes. [6.] Great mystery. There are phenomena in nature which cannot be solved, secrets which cannot be fathomed nor accounted for. But from what we see of heaven and earth we may easily enough infer the eternal power and God head of the great Creator, and may furnish ourselves with abundant matter for his praises. And let our make and place, as men, remind us of our duty as Christians, which is always to keep heaven in our eye and the earth under our feet."

Matthew Henry *Commentary*

For Reflection and Reasoning

• Review the pictures in the Student Text which reveal God's character — the variety of His creation, His beauty and His power.

• If we look at the plants, how many different kinds of plants can we find? If we look at the birds, how many kinds of birds can we see? If we look at the fish in the sea, how many kinds of fish are there? How many different kinds of animals can you name?

• Creation teaches us about God. What do the beautiful animals, plants, birds, and fish teach us about God? What does a beautiful sky or sunset teach us about God? Have you seen tall mountains? Are they also beautiful?

• Look at books of animals, birds, or fish and discuss the variety seen in the creation. Observe their physical characteristics, habits, or nature.

• Use *Student Activity Page 5-4*. Reason from the Student Text to record the characteristics of God revealed in creation. Students could paste or draw pictures of animals, birds, fish, etc., on the bottom of the page.

> **Creation teaches us many things about God.**
>
> Variety
>
> Beauty
>
> Power

• Have you seen the great waves in the oceans or seas? Have you heard the mighty thunder or seen the lightning? Since God controls the winds and the waves, what does this show about His power?

Chapter 6
God Created the Continents
3-5 Days

> **Leading Idea**
>
> ## God created each continent for a unique purpose: Asia
>
> Student Text, pages 17-18

• Continent — "In *geography*, a great extent of land, not disjoined or interrupted by a sea; a connected tract of land of great extent; as the Eastern and Western *continent*. It differs from an isle only in extent."

• Each continent has a unique shape and purpose. Geographer Arnold Guyot identified the role geography played in history, with the design of each continent best fitting it for a particular contribution. He identified Asia as the "continent of origins," Europe as the "continent of development," and America as "destined to furnish the most complete expression of the Christian civilization." The southern continents provide the greatest expressions of nature.[7]

For Reflection and Reasoning

• What is a continent? Can you identify each continent on a globe or map of the world?

• As you read each section on the individual continents, look at a globe or map to identify the geographic characteristics of that continent.

• Which is the largest continent? Which continent seems closer to all of the other continents? On which continent did God place Adam and Eve when they were created? On which continent did Christ live when He came to earth?

• Use a globe or world map to identify the unique geographic characteristics of Asia. You may wish to point out the location of major mountain regions and how that would have affected travel in the continents, and encouraged the spread of Christianity.

• Using *Student Activity Page 6-1*, students outline and label each continent as it is studied to see the distinctives of the border. If inadequate time, the students could outline and label only the northern continents. An alternate plan would be to use construction paper to cut out the shape of each continent and paste each continent on a separate sheet, labeling the name of the continent at the top. See *Student Activity Page 6-2*.

 **Leading Idea**

God created each continent for a unique purpose: Europe

Student Text, page 18

For Reflection and Reasoning

• Which continent has more coastline than any other? How would it help people to travel or communicate if there is more coastline and lower mountains?

• Students continue labeling and outlining world map, *Student Activity Page 6-1* or *Student Activity Page 6-3.*

 **Leading Idea**

God created each continent for a unique purpose: North America

Student Text, page 19

For Reflection and Reasoning

• How is North America very different from Europe and Asia? What kept people from finding North America for so many years? Why would God have wanted to keep North America from being settled?

• How would the geography of the northern continents help to move Chris-tianity from Asia through Europe to North America?

• Why would the individual have more liberty if a nation is based upon the Bible?

• Students continue labeling and outlining world map, *Student Activity Page 6-1* or *Student Activity Page 6-4.*

Leading Idea

God created each continent for a unique purpose: Australia, Africa, South America and Antarctica

Student Text, pages 20-22

For Reflection and Reasoning

• When you look at the globe or a map, can you see how there are pairs of continents? What pairs can you identify?

• What continent is the partner to Asia?

• Consider the pictures in the Student Text. What rare animals and plants live in Australia?

   Note: The picture includes the bottle tree, acacias, eucalyptus, ants, anteater, koala, platypus, crocodile, emus, kangaroos, kookaburra, and cockatoo. (Ants are represented by ant mounds.)

• What continent is the partner to Europe?

• What grand kinds of animals live in Africa?

• What continent is the partner to North America?

• South America has what is called *rain forests*. How would this help to produce the beautiful plants? Consider the picture in the Student Text.

• Locate the continent of Antarctica on a globe. Why would we say that Antarctica is at the South Pole? Where is the North Pole?

• Consider the picture in the Student Text. Are there many animals living on Antarctica? Why or why not?

• Students continue labeling and outlining world map, *Student Activity Page 6-1* or *Student Activity Pages 6-5, 6-6, and 6-7.*

Chapter 7
God Created Man
3-4 Days

God created man in His own image.

Student Text, pages 23-24

• "That man's creation was a more signal and immediate act of divine wisdom and power than that of the other creatures. The narrative of it is introduced with something of solemnity, and a manifest distinction from the rest. Hitherto, it had been said, 'Let there be light,' and 'Let there be a firmament,' and 'Let the earth, or waters, bring forth' such a thing; but now the word of command is turned into a word of consultation, '*Let us make man,* for whose sake the rest of the creatures were made: this is a work we must take into our own hands.' . . . Man was to be a creature different from all that had been hitherto made. Flesh and spirit, heaven and earth, must be put together in him, and he must be allied to both worlds. And therefore God himself not only undertakes to make him, but is pleased so to express himself as if he called a council to consider of the making of him: *Let us make man.* The three persons of the Trinity, Father, Son, and Holy Ghost, consult about it and concur in it, because man, when he was made, was to be dedicated and devoted to Father, Son, and Holy Ghost. . .

"That man was made in God's image and after his likeness, two words to express the same thing and making each other the more expressive; *image* and *likeness* denote the likest image, the nearest resemblance of any of the visible creatures. Man was not made in the likeness of any creature that went before him, but in the likeness of his Creator; yet still between God and man there is an infinite distance. Christ only is the *express* image of God's person, as the Son of his Father, having the same nature. It is only some of God's honour that is put upon man, who is God's image only as the shadow in the glass, or the king's impress upon the coin. God's image upon man consists in these three things:—1. In his nature and constitution, not those of his body (for God has not a body), but those of his soul . . . It is the soul, the great soul, of man, that does especially bear God's image. . . 2. In his place and authority: *Let us make man in our image, and let him have dominion.* As he has the government of the inferior creatures, he is, as it were, God's representative, or viceroy, upon earth; they are not capable of fearing and serving God, therefore God has appointed them to fear and serve man. Yet his government of himself by the freedom of his will has in it more of God's image than his government of the creatures. 3. In his purity and rectitude. God's image upon man consists in knowledge, righteousness, and true holiness, Eph. iv. 24; Col. iii. 10. He was upright. Eccl. vii. 29. . . . Thus holy, thus happy, were our first parents, in having the image of God upon them. And this honour, put upon man at first, is a good reason why we should not speak ill one of another (Jam. iii. 9), nor do ill one to another (Gen. ix. 6), and a good reason why we should not debase ourselves to the service of sin, and why we should devote ourselves to God's service . . ."

Matthew Henry *Commentary*

For Reflection and Reasoning

• Review: What does it mean to create?

• Read Genesis 1:26-27.

• Using Student Text, identify how man is different from the rest of God's creation? Students may copy these distinctives into the Student Notes.

• What does it mean to be created in God's image?

• How does each person in your family show the variety of God's creation? Are you exactly like any other person? Each student may draw a picture of his family, showing how each individual is different.

> **Leading Idea**
>
> # Man was made to glorify God.
>
> Student Text, page 24

• Consider the Scriptures which teach that man was made to glorify God:

Isaiah 43:7, 21; Rev. 4:11; Eph. 1:6, 12.

For Reflection and Reasoning

• Why was man made?

• How can man glorify God?

• Sing songs: *Praise Him, Praise Him;*

Thou Art Worthy; Doxology.

Suggested Student Notes

Man was made to glorify God.

> **Leading Idea**
>
> # Man is God's property.
>
> Student Text, pages 25-26

• By right of the creation, man belongs to God. Ephesians 2:10 teaches us "For we are all his workmanship, created in Christ Jesus unto good works, which God hath before ordained that we should walk in them."

• Consider Scriptures which teach that

the earth and all that is in it belong to God, i.e. Deuteronomy 10:14; Psalm 24:1.

• I Samuel 2:6 teaches us that God controls the length of our life. "The Lord killeth, and maketh alive: he bringeth down to the grave, and bringeth up."

• God created each individual. He has a plan and purpose for each person which He created. He also gave man responsibility for the earth, to care for it. Man has a stewardship responsibility for all that God has given him, whether internal talents or ideas, or external houses, lands, or wealth.

For Reflection and Reasoning

• Review: Who created you? Why were you made?

• What is your responsibility or duty?

• History reveals that God uses individuals to fulfill His plan in history.

• God has a plan for each of you in His Story.

• Sing Songs: *He Owns the Cattle on a Thousand Hills; This is my Father's World; I am Thine.*

Leading Idea

Sin changed man's relationship to God.

Student Text, p. 26

• When Adam and Eve ate of the tree of the knowledge of good and evil, they disobeyed God. This disobedience was sin and separated them from God.

"God put marks of his displeasure on Adam in three instances: —

"1. His habitation is, by this sentence, cursed: . . . It is here intimated that his habitation should be changed; he should no longer dwell in a distinguished, blessed, paradise, but should be removed to common ground, and that cursed . . .

"2. His employments and enjoyments are all embittered to him. (1.) His business shall henceforth become a toil to him, and he shall go on with it *in the sweat of his face, v.* 19. . . .(2) His food shall henceforth become (in comparison with what it had been) unpleasant to him. . .

"3. His life also is but short. . . (3.) That sin brought death into the world. If Adam had not sinned, he would not have died, Rom. v. 12. God entrusted Adam with a spark of immortality, which he, by a patient continuance in well-doing, might have blown up into an everlasting flame; but he foolishly blew it out by wilful sin: and now death is *the wages of* sin, and *sin is the sting of death.*"

Matthew Henry *Commentary*

• Roman 5:12 teaches us "Wherefore, as by one man sin entered into the world, and death by sin; and so death passed upon all men, for that all have sinned:"

For Reflection and Reasoning

• What is sin? When did sin come into the world? What is the result of that sin?

• How were Adam and Eve governed differently after they sinned? Why did they need to be governed differently?

• Depending on the students knowledge of Adam and Eve's sin, the story can be reviewed from memory, or selected verses could be read from Genesis 3.

• See *Student Activity Page 7-1*. Using the Student Text, identify how sin changed man's walk with God.

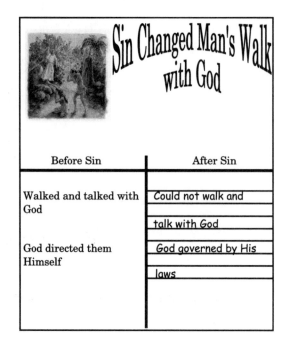

Before Sin	After Sin
Walked and talked with God	Could not walk and
	talk with God
God directed them Himself	God governed by His
	laws

MOSES

1-2 Weeks

Chapter 8
Moses and the Law

1-2 Weeks

• Exodus 1:8 sets the stage for the study of Moses. "There arose up a new king over Egypt, which knew not Joseph." Matthew Henry expands the setting: "The land of Egypt here, at length, becomes to Israel a house of bondage, though hitherto it had been a happy shelter and settlement for them. . . . I. The obligations they lay under to Israel upon Joseph's account were forgotten: . . . All that knew him loved him, and were kind to his relations for his sake; but when he was dead he was soon forgotten, and the remembrance of the good offices he had done was either not retained or not regarded, nor had it any influence upon their councils."

• In I Samuel 8, the Lord reminded the Children of Israel of the manner of kings that reign. The King of Egypt, Pharaoh by name, demonstrated the unlimited power of a king.

For Reflection and Reasoning

• Briefly relate the story of the Children of Israel being led to Egypt.

• Locate Egypt on a map.

• Show pictures of pyramids, sphinx or other Egyptian structures.

• What is a king? Pharaoh was the king of Egypt. Pharaoh could make any laws he wanted.

• Why was Pharaoh afraid of the Children of Israel?

• Using the Student Text, have the students identify how Pharaoh was unjust.

• Reflect upon the picture on page 27 of the Student Text, and the difficult tasks being done. Relate this to the difficult tasks given to the Children of Israel.

Leading Idea

Moses was protected by God for His purpose.

Student Text, page 28

• "Here is, I. Moses saved from perishing. . . . Had he been left to lie there, he must have perished in a little time with hunger, if he had not been sooner washed into the river or devoured by a crocodile. Had he fallen into any other hands than those he did fall into, either they would not, or durst not, have done otherwise than have thrown him straightway into the river; but Providence brings no less a person thither than Pharaoh's daughter, just at that juncture, guides her to the place where this poor forlorn infant lay, and inclines her heart to pity it, which she dares do when none else durst. Never did poor child cry so seasonably, so happily, as this did: *The babe wept*, which moved the compassion of the princess. . . 4. God often raises up friends for his people even among their enemies. Pharaoh cruelly seeks Israel's destruction, but his own daughter charitably compassionates a Hebrew child, and not only so, but, beyond her intention, preserves Israel's deliverer. *O Lord, how wonderful are thy counsels!"*

Matthew Henry *Commentary*

For Reflection and Reasoning

• Review: What is Providence?

• Read selected verses from Exodus 2:1-10 to review the story of Moses.

• How can we see God's Providence in protecting Moses? Consider: 1) The king's laws; and 2) It was Pharaoh's own daughter that protected Moses.

• Color the picture of Pharaoh's daughter finding Moses, *Student Activity Page 8-1.* Student notes may be recorded on activity page.

God cared for baby Moses.

Suggested Student Notes

God cared for baby Moses.

Leading Idea

Moses was used by God as Deliverer.

Student Text, pages 29-30

• Review Exodus, chapters 3-13.

• God heard the Children of Israel's cry

of the injustice of Pharaoh, and called Moses to lead them from Egypt.

• Webster defines a deliverer as "one who releases or rescues; a preserver."

God used Moses to be that deliverer. But He was still guiding — He sent the pillar of cloud and the pillar of fire to lead them on their path.

For Reflection and Reasoning

• Why were the Children of Israel unhappy in Egypt?

• How did Pharaoh's speech reveal that he did not want to hear what God wanted him to do?

• What does it mean to be a deliverer? How did God use Moses to be the deliverer of the Children of Israel?

• Look at a map to identify Egypt, the wilderness, and Israel. A good map is included in the Thompson Chain Reference Bible.

• God used Moses in several positions.

On *Student Activity Page 8-2*, record "Deliverer" and a definition of *Deliverer*, "leads people from an enemy." Remainder of chart will be completed in the following lessons.

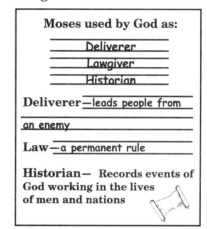

Moses used by God as:

Deliverer

Lawgiver

Historian

Deliverer—leads people from an enemy

Law—a permanent rule

Historian— Records events of God working in the lives of men and nations

> **Leading Idea**
>
> *"The king's heart is in the hand of the Lord." Proverbs 21:1*

• The purpose of this study is not to detail the events of God's dealing with Pharaoh and Egypt, but to see God's control of the events.

• "Note, 1. Even the *hearts* of men are in God's hand, and not only their *goings*, as he had said, ch. xx. 24. God can change men's minds, can, by a powerful insensible operation upon their spirits, turn them from that which they seemed most intent upon, and incline them to that which they seemed most averse to, as the husbandman, by canals and gutters, turns the water through his grounds as he pleases, which does not alter the nature of the water, nor put any force upon it, any more than God's

providence does upon the native freedom of man's will, but directs the course of it to serve his own purpose.

"2. Even kings' hearts are so, notwithstanding their powers and prerogatives, as much as the hearts of common persons. The *hearts of kings are unsearchable* to us, much more unmanageable by us; as they have their *arcana imperii — state secrets*, so they have the prerogatives of their crown; but the great God has them not only under his eye, but in his hand. Kings are what he makes them. Those that are most absolute are under God's government; he *puts things into their hearts*, Rev. xvii. 17; Ezra vii. 27."

Matthew Henry, *Commentary*

• *"The king's heart*; his very inward purposes and inclinations, which seem to be most in a man's own power, and out of the reach of all others, and much more his tongue and hand, and all his outward actions. He names *kings* not to exclude other men, but because they are more arbitrary and uncontrollable than other men. *As the rivers of water*; which husbandmen or gardeners can draw by little channels into the adjacent grounds as they please, and as their occasions require. *He turneth it*; directeth and boweth, partly by suggesting those things to their minds which have a commanding influence upon their wills; and partly by a direct and immediate motion of their wills and affections, which being God's creatures must needs be as subject to his power and pleasure as either men's minds or bodies are, and which he moves sweetly and suitably to

their own nature, though strongly and effectually. *Whithersoever he will*; so as they shall fulfill his counsels and designs, either of mercy or of correction to themselves, or to their people."
Matthew Poole, *A Commentary on the Holy Bible*

• "God alone knows the true heart of a man, I Samuel 16:7. If History and, indeed, if men and nations are to be progressive and to go forward, they must all depend upon Providence to work mightily in the unseen, unknown centers of human activity, to direct, regulate, control, and restrain the powers which would otherwise impede or pull backward. God, by His Providence, works invisibly, internally, imperceptibly and individually within men and nations."[8]
Katherine Dang, *Universal History*

For Reflection and Reasoning

• Using *Student Activity Pages 8-3* and *8-4*, review the events of God's allowing the Children of Israel to leave Egypt. The emphasis is to see God's control and how *The king's heart is in the hand of the Lord.* Cut and glue pictures of Moses. Students may draw a scroll in the box to represent the unjust laws and a heart to represent Pharoah's changed heart.

• What does it mean to "soften the heart"? How did God "soften" Pharaoh's heart? How does this show us that the king's heart was in "the hand of the Lord"?

• When Moses did not think he could go to Pharaoh, what did God do for him?

• The Children of Israel traveled from Egypt back to the Promised Land. How did they know what path to take?

 **Leading Idea** — *Since man is a sinner, he requires external law.*

• Since man is a sinner, he requires external law. Man must be governed, either by a power within or a power without.

• Webster defines a law as "A rule, particularly an established or permanent rule, prescribed by the supreme power of

a state to its subjects, for regulating their actions. . ."

• A simple, student definition might be "A permanent rule." Students understand rules at home, rules in the classroom, etc.

For Reflection and Reasoning

• What is a law? What does permanent mean? Why do we need laws?

• What are some laws we must obey? In your home? In the car? At a store?

• Are laws internal or external government?

• Review the idea of internal and external government. See Teacher's Guide, pages 21-22.

• On *Student Activity Page 8-2*, record a definition of *Law*, "A permanent rule."

Cultivating Student Mastery

1. What is a deliverer?

2. What is a law?

Leading Idea

Moses was used by God as Lawgiver.

Student Text, pages 30-32

• God chose Moses to be the one who would bring His law to the people. Exodus 31:18 tells us that these tables of stone were "written with the finger of God."

• The law given by God to Moses involved moral law, civil law, and ritual law. For the purpose of this study and the age of student, it would be best to mention only the moral law, or the ten commandments. Webster defines moral law as "a law which prescribes to men their religious and social duties, in other words, their duties to God and to each other. The moral law is summarily contained in the decalogue or ten commandments, written by the finger of God on two tables of stone, and delivered to Moses on mount Sinai. Ex. xx."

For Reflection and Reasoning

• How was the law written? God Himself wrote in stone with His finger.

• The laws given to Moses identify specific rules to govern our relationship to God and our relationship to other people.

• Selected verses from Exodus 20:1-17 may be read to identify the type of laws given — those which control our relationship to God and those which control our relationship to man. In a later year, these laws will be addressed more specifically.

• How are laws made today? Laws that are made today should be based upon the laws which God gave.

• Color the picture of Moses and the stone tablets. *Student Activity Page 8-5.*

• On *Student Activity Page 8-2*, record "Lawgiver."

Cultivating Student Mastery

1. Why did man need the written law?

Leading Idea

Moses used by God as first Historian

Student Text, page 32

• Webster describes an historian as "A writer or compiler of history; one who collects and relates facts and events in writing, particularly respecting nations." A Providential historian would record events of God working in the lives of men and nations.

• Exodus 17:14—"And the Lord said unto Moses, Write this *for* a memorial in a book, and rehearse *it* in the ears of Joshua. . ."

• "We have before us that part of the Old Testament which we call the *Pentateuch,* or five books of Moses. . . In our Saviour's distribution of the books of the Old Testament into the *law,* the *prophets,* and the *psalms,* these are the *law;*

for they contain not only the laws given to Israel, in the last four, but the laws given to Adam, to Noah, and to Abraham, in the first. These five books were, for aught we know, the first that ever were written; for we have not the least mention of any *writing* in all the book of Genesis, nor till God bade Moses write (Exod. xvii. 14); and some think Moses himself never learned to write till God set him his copy in the writing of the Ten Commandments upon the tables of stone. However, we are sure these books are the most ancient writings now extant, and therefore best able to give us a satisfactory account of the most ancient things."

Matthew Henry *Commentary*

For Reflection and Reasoning

• Review: What is history? Why do we study history? How do we learn history? How does history help us to remember what God has done? See Teacher's Guide, pages 17-18.

• On *Student Activity Page 8-2,* record "Historian." Review definition of historian.

• How do we know about creation, of Adam and Eve, and Moses?

• Look at several history books and identify how they cover different periods of time.

• Moses wrote the first five books of the Bible — Genesis, Exodus, Leviticus, Numbers, and Deuteronomy. Can you

find these books in your Bible?

• In what book do we find the record of creation? Where can we read the record of Adam and Eve? Where do we find the record of the Children of Israel leaving Egypt?

• Moses recorded history from creation through the end of his life, a period of over 2000 years. (According to Ussher's chronology: 4004 B.C. to 1451 B.C.)

• On *Student Activity Page 8-6,* record "Moses was the first historian."

Cultivating Student Mastery

1. What is an historian?

2. Who was the first historian?

CHRIST
The Focal Point of History
1 Week

Chapter 9
Christ Changed History
1 Week

Leading Idea

In the fulness of time, Christ came.

Student Text, page 33

• *"When the fulness of time had come,* the time appointed of the Father, when he would put an end to the legal dispensation, and set up another and a better in the room of it, *he sent forth his Son, &c.* The person who was employed to introduce this new dispensation was no other than the Son of God himself, the only begotten of the Father, who, as he had been prophesied of and promised from the foundation of the world, so in due time he was manifested for this purpose. He, in pursuance of the great design he had undertaken, submitted to be *made of a woman*—there is his incarnation; and to be *made under the law*—there is his subjection. He who was truly God for our sakes became man; and he who was Lord of all consented to come into a state of subjection and to take upon him the form of a servant; and one great end of all this was *to redeem those that were under the law*—to save us from that intolerable yoke and to appoint gospel ordinances more rational and easy. . .”

Matthew Henry *Commentary*

• The Roman Empire was man's best effort to establish a nation. Yet Rome was crumbling. When man's greatest effort in civil government had failed, man was ready for the Saviour.

For Reflection and Reasoning

• Review: When did time begin? How long has God been?

• Galatians 4:4 tells us that "when the fulness of time was come, God sent forth his son."

• The Bible is divided into two sections. What are these two sections? What event separates the two sections of the Bible? We call these two sections the Old Testament and New Testament.

The Old Testament looked forward to Christ's coming. The New Testament tells of His coming and the effect of the Gospel in men's hearts and lives.

• On the Board, begin to develop a chart illustrating Christ as the focal point of history. See *Student Activity Page 9-1*. This may be completed by the student for his notebook. Label Old Testament, New Testament, and Christ. Remainder of chart will be completed in the following lessons.

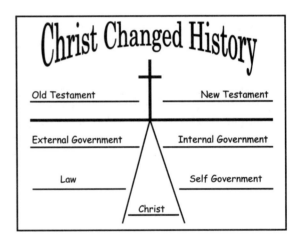

 **Leading Idea**

Unto you is born a Saviour.

Student Text, pages 33-34

• Webster defines a *Savior* as "One that saves or preserves; but properly applied only to Jesus Christ, the Redeemer, who has opened the way to everlasting salvation by his obedience and death, and who is therefore called *the Savior,* by way of distinction, the *Savior* of men, the *Savior* of the world."

For Reflection and Reasoning

• Read selected passage of Scripture, perhaps sections of Luke 2, which recount the events of Christ's birth.

• Review briefly the wonderful story of Christ's birth. Identify the special events which remind us that Jesus was God's Son, who came to earth to provide salvation for each individual.

• Sing songs of Jesus birth: *Joy to the World; Away in a Manger.*

• Color a picture of the nativity scene. See *Student Activity Page 9-2.*

Christ came to change the hearts of men.

Student Text, pages 34-35

• Romans 3:23 reminds us: "For all have sinned and come short of the glory of God."

• Christ came to provide redemption for each individual. Webster defines redemption: "In *theology*, the purchase of God's favor by the death and sufferings of Christ; the ransom or deliverance of sinners from the bondage of sin and the penalties of God's violated law by the atonement of Christ."

• Redemption can only be provided through the shedding of blood. Christ shed His blood for our redemption. See Ephesians 1:7 and Colossians 1:14 .

For Reflection and Reasoning

• What is salvation? How can we have salvation? Review John 3:16.

• Why did Christ come to the earth? What did it cost Him to provide salvation for us?

• Sing songs of salvation: *For God so Loved the World; The Old Rugged Cross;* *Nothing but the Blood.*

Suggested Student Notes

Christ came to change men's hearts.

Christ made internal, Christian self government, possible.

Student Text, pages 35-36

• As the individual accepts the gift of salvation, an internal change occurs. The relationship between God and the individual is changed. Christ indwells the heart of the believer.

• As Christ dwells in an individual's heart, He desires to control every action. This occurs only as we consent to His control. Only as we follow Christ and the Word of God and are obedient to Him will we have internal, Christian self-government.

For Reflection and Reasoning

• Review the definition of government. Why is it necessary to have Christ within us in order to be self governed?

• *Student Activity Page 9-1.* Label External Government and Law. Label Internal Government and Self Government. Reason with the students concerning the internal change of Christ governing our hearts. With Christ's coming, man has the opportunity to be controlled and directed (governed) by Christ—internally.

• Review the poem from Student Text, Chapter 2, *My Kingdom.*

• If we have Christ internally, how will it affect the way we live?

• On the Board, illustrate the governmental idea that as we govern ourselves we have Christian self government. When we have Christian self government, we are then prepared to govern our family. Once we can govern a family, we will be prepared to govern in the local, state, and national government.

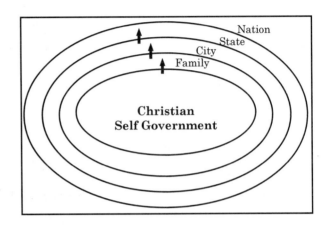

• Consider the many centuries that it took for people to recognize that if they could govern themselves and their own family, they, too, could govern their own cities, states, and nations.

• Why did the people need the Bible in their hands before they understood the ideas about civil government?

PAUL

1 Week

Chapter 10
Apostle Paul
Link to Europe
1 Week

┌───┐
│ ⭑*Leading Idea*⭑   **God uses individuals to**   │
│   **accomplish His plan.**   │
│   │
│   Student Text, pages 37-38   │
└───┘

• God's plan was for the Gospel to be taken westward to Europe. Paul was thinking of going to Bithynia to preach, but God showed him that he should go to Macedonia. Paul obeyed God's instruction and God blessed his labors. People came to know of salvation, many believed in Jesus, and churches were established in several European cities.

• Consider the Scriptural account of Paul's call into Macedonia and his labors in Europe, beginning with Acts 16.

• For the purpose of the elementary history course, it would be best not to elaborate upon the details of Paul's missionary journeys. Such a study would be excellent in a Bible class.

For Reflection and Reasoning

• Review: What is the Gospel? Why is the Gospel "good news?" Who preached the Gospel in Asia?

• Why would the first churches have

been formed in Asia? On what continent did Christ live and die?

• Why did Paul decide to go to Macedonia? On what continent is Macedonia?

• For this particular study, the emphasis must be placed on the movement of Christianity from Asia to Europe, not on the specific cities visited by Paul. The details of this journey are identified in Acts, beginning in Chapter 16. Most Bibles include maps, which would identify the route of Paul's journey.

• Read selected verses from Acts 16.

• Begin a map, showing the spread of the Gospel from Asia to Europe. *Student Activity Page 10-1.* Label and outline Asia. See *Map Instructions,* Teacher's Guide, page 10.

Leading Idea

God prepared the people of Europe to receive the Gospel.

Student Text, page 38

• In God's Providence, He prepared the hearts of the people who heard Paul preach. Some, like Lydia, were anxious to hear the Gospel and tell others. Even in difficult circumstances, Paul was always ready to tell people how Jesus Christ could change their hearts and lives. Example: The Philippian jailer, Acts 16:25-34.

• Christ, during his ministry, traveled in Asia preaching and teaching. God wanted the message of Christianity to be preached and taught to the people of Europe, in the same way.

Christianity recognizes the importance and value of the individual. The Apostles took the message to each person who would listen. It did not matter if a person was young or old, a man or a woman, a servant or a master. It did not matter whether one person would listen, or a few, or a whole crowd. The Apostles patiently preached the Gospel and many received their teaching with joy and gladness.

For Reflection and Reasoning

• In the days of Paul, how could any man, woman, boy, or girl have heard about Christ and that He had died for their sins?

• How did Paul travel to Europe? Would it have taken Paul longer to travel from Asia to Europe than it would if you made the trip today? Why?

• Who was the first Christian in Europe? Paul obeyed God, but who was responsible for people accepting Christ?

• Continue map work: Label and outline Europe.

Leading Idea

Christianity moved westward

Student Text, pages 38-40

• Christianity began, geographically, on the continent of Asia. God, in his infinite wisdom, saw fit to move the Gospel to Europe, from where it began its westward journey, eventually coming to North America and being the basis of the United States of America.

• Consider the links God used to move the Gospel westward, see Teacher's Guide, page 31.

• Name two ways God's Providence is shown in this chapter.

• Earlier this year we discussed Christianity's westward movement. What did we learn about each link on a chain?

• Paul wrote many books of the New Testament. Can you find one?

• Why would Paul be called the "link" to Europe?

• Continue map work: Color the arrows showing the westward movement. Title the map: "Apostle Paul: Link to Europe."

• Color the picture of Paul writing his letters, which would become part of the New Testament. *Student Activity Page 10-2.*

THE BIBLE IN ENGLISH
2-3 Weeks

Chapter 11
A Bible for the People
2-3 Weeks

> ### Leading Idea
>
> ### *The Bible is inspired by God and recorded by men.*
>
> Student Text, page 41

• "For the prophecy came not in old time by the will of man: but holy men of God spake as they were moved by the Holy Ghost." II Peter 1:21.

• "Observe, (1.) They were holy men of God who were employed about that book which we receive as the word of God. . . All the penmen of the scriptures were holy men of God. (2.) *These holy men were moved by the Holy Ghost* in what they delivered as the mind and will of God. The Holy Ghost is the supreme agent, the holy men are but instruments. [1.] The Holy Ghost inspired and dictated to them what they were to deliver of the mind of God. [2.] He powerfully excited and effectually engaged them to speak (and write) what he had put into their mouths. [3.] He so wisely and carefully assisted and directed them in the delivery of what they had received from him that they were effectually secured from any the least mistake in expressing what they revealed; so that the very words of scripture are to be accounted the words of the Holy Ghost, and all the plainness and simplicity, all the power and virtue, all the elegance and propriety, of the very words and expressions are to be regarded by us as proceeding from God. Mix faith therefore with what you find in the scriptures; esteem and reverence your Bible as a book written by holy men, inspired, influenced, and assisted by the Holy Ghost."
Matthew Henry *Commentary*

For Reflection and Reasoning

• Review: Who recorded the first books of the Bible? What books did he record?

• Review: Paul recorded many books of the New Testament. What were some of the books that were written by Paul? How do we know most of the books written by Paul?

• If the topic of the inspiration of the Scripture was previously covered in Bible class, this lesson should be a review of the ideas previously taught.

• Read together II Peter 1:21. All or a portion of this verse could be recorded by the student.

• God used many different individuals to record the Scriptures. The canon of Scripture was written over a period of over 1,000 years, with the last book being recorded approximately 90 A.D.

• How did Moses, Paul, Matthew, Mark, Luke, and John know what words to record?

• What kind of men would God want to use to record His Word? Why?

• Did these men have paper and pens? What did they use to record the words which God gave to them?

• Demonstrate writing with a quill. Remind the students that the Scriptures were first written on scrolls.

• What language do we speak? In what language was the Bible originally written? What would happen if our Bibles were still in those languages?

• Show the students a sample of Scriptures written in another language. Help them understand the importance of having the Bible in their language.

• Sing some songs which identify the importance of the Word of God. Examples: *The B-I-B-L-E; The Book of Books; The Bible Stands.* You may enjoy teaching one new song during the study of this chapter.

• See *Student Activity Page 11-1*. Read and discuss the poem, *How Precious is the Book Divine*.

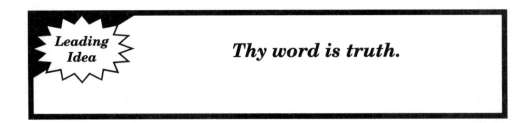

Leading Idea

Thy word is truth.

• John 14:6 teaches that Jesus Christ is the truth. All truth must come from God and His Word. Therefore, without the Word of God, there will be error.

• Webster tells us that truth is

"Conformity to fact or reality; exact accordance with that which is, or has been, or shall be. . . We rely on the *truth* of the scriptural prophecies." Error, therefore, is "A wandering or deviation from the truth; . . ."

For Reflection and Reasoning

• Read and discuss John 14:6.

• What is truth? If something is not true, what is it?

• If God's Word is truth and all truth comes from His Word, why is it important for each person to have a Bible?

• Use *Student Activity Page 11-2*. Write on scroll: "...thy word is truth." John 17:17b.

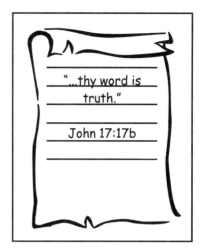

"...thy word is truth."

John 17:17b

Leading Idea

Without the Bible, truth will be hidden.

Student Text, pages 41-42

• In New Testament times, God used the Apostles, particularly Paul, to teach and preach throughout Asia and Europe. As they ministered in these areas, churches were formed. Historians describe these churches in different ways. Leonard Bacon, in his *Genesis of the New England Churches*, 1874, described the first century churches: "there are indications that in every place the society of believers in Christ was a little republic. . . Each local church was complete in itself, and was held responsible to Christ for its own character, and the character of those whom it retained in its fellowship."[9]

• Between the first century after Christ to the time of Constantine (312 A.D.), changes occurred in the structure of the churches. The self-governing churches of the first century gradually changed to an Episcopal form of church government, with power flowing from the top down. The power gradually centered in the Church of Rome. Constantine set himself as the head of that church in 312 A.D. This Church dominated history for centuries until the Reformation.

These changes occurred because people did not have access to the Bible, and could not know the Scriptural principles of church government.

For Reflection and Reasoning

• Look at a map of the Roman Empire to see the extent of control held by the Roman Church.

• Consider the government of the first century church. Each church was an independent ministry.

• Use *Student Activity Page 11-3*.

Discuss that the New Testament churches were independent and self governing. Students may draw a cross on each church. Draw a line from each church to the Roman Church to illustrate the relationship which developed between Rome and the other churches.

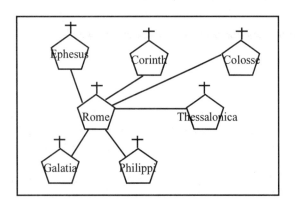

• Use *Student Activity Pages 11-4* and *11-5* to begin a timeline, *A Bible for the People.* Record: "The Bible was not in English." Remainder of timeline will be completed in the following lessons.

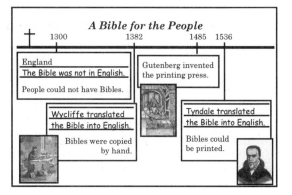

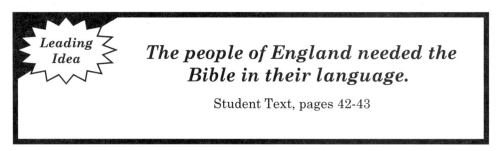

Leading Idea	*The people of England needed the Bible in their language.*

Student Text, pages 42-43

• Until 1382, the Scriptures were not available to the individual. This period of history was called the Dark Ages. It was dark, since Scriptures were not available to give light.

• The Roman Church retained the Scriptures in their possession. However, they would not allow the people to have copies of the Bible. Laws were made which made it illegal to own a Bible.

For Reflection and Reasoning

• Review: In what language was the Old Testament first written? The New Testament?

• Review: Under the Roman Church, into what language was the Bible translated? What language did the people of England speak?

• Why did the people of England not have the Bible?

• What does translate mean?

• From what language did John Wycliffe translate the Bible?

Cultivating Student Mastery

1. Why did John Wycliffe want to translate the Bible for the people of England?

Leading Idea

God used John Wycliffe to provide a Bible for the people of England.

Student Text, pages 43-44

• After Wycliffe's death, the church authorities hoped that interest in the work of Wycliffe would become extinct. However, Wycliffe's followers, called Lollards, enthusiastically continued their work to spread the Word of God throughout England.

The name of Lollard was a term of derision, meaning babbler.

The major distribution of the Scripture was through religious tracts, and through portions of the Scripture.

• History appears to reveal a correlation between the love of the Word of God and the scholarship of the people. As people want to read the Bible, they must learn to read for themselves.

For Reflection and Reasoning

• Why did the people of England not have many books? Why were they not able to read?

• The followers of Wycliffe, the Lollards, began to teach the people to read. The people wanted to read so they could read the Bible.

• Name several ways in which the Bible changed people's lives.

• How were the Lollards able to spread the Gospel in England?

• Use *Student Activity Pages 11-4* and *11-5*. Continue the timeline, *A Bible for the People*. Students cut and glue the picture of Wycliffe. Record: "Wycliffe translated the Bible into English."

• Have the students record a small portion of Scripture in the form of a tract. Suggested verses: Isaiah 40:4b or John 17:17b. Emphasize the labor involved in all Scriptures being copied by hand and the work of the Lollards in distributing the tracts.

The design of the Lollard's tracts is unknown. The following is an idea: Use about 1/2 sheet of student lined paper. Have the student copy a verse from the Bible onto the page. Fold the paper in half and the reference for the verse might be put on the outside.

If time permits, the student could decorate the front of the tract or make a border around the verse.

The student could be encouraged to share this tract with a friend, student from another class, or family member.

Note: This activity would probably consume one class time.

Leading Idea

The history of the Bible is the history of printing.

Student Text, pages 44-46

• Historian Philip Schaff makes the correlation between the history of the Bible and the history of printing: "The Bible is the common property and most sacred treasure of all Christian churches. Henry Stevens says (*The Bibles in the Caxton Exhibition,* p. 25): 'The secular history of the Holy Scriptures is the sacred history of Printing. The Bible was the first book printed and the Bible is the last book printed. Between 1450 and 1877, an interval of four centuries and a quarter, the Bible shows the progress and comparative development of the art of printing in a manner that no other single book can; and Biblical bibliography proves that during the first forty years, at least, the Bible exceeded in amount of printing all other books put together; nor were its quality, style, and variety a whit behind its quantity.'

". . . The art of printing, which was one of the providential preparations for the Reformation, became the mightiest lever of Protestantism and modern culture. . .

"Thus, with the freedom of conscience, was born the freedom of the press. But it had to pass through a severe ordeal, even in Protestant countries, and was constantly checked by Roman authorities as far as their power extended."[10]

Philip Schaff, *History of the Christian Church*

• For further study on the history of printing, see *A Guide to American Christian Education,* pages 489-490, "Typing in the American Christian Curriculum," by Barbara Rose.

For Reflection and Reasoning

• Review: How was John Wycliffe's translation of the Bible prepared for the people? Would a printing press help to spread the Word of God? How?

• Prior to Gutenberg's press, printing was a very difficult, slow process. Identify for the students the difference in producing a book with movable type.

Using the illustration in the Student Text, page 46, identify the process of producing a page on a press like Gutenberg's. Why is it called a printing "press"?

• Locate Germany on a map. The people of England had been reading the Bible from Wycliffe's translation, when God raised up Gutenberg in Germany to produce the printing press.

• How did Gutenberg's invention make it possible for more people to have the Bible?

• Use *Student Activity Pages 11-4* and *11-5,* continue the timeline, *A Bible for the People.* Cut and glue picture of Gutenberg's printing press.

Cultivating Student Mastery

1. How was Johannes Gutenberg used to spread the Gospel?

Leading Idea

"I will cause a boy that driveth a plow to know more of the Scriptures than the pope."

Student Text, pages 46-47

• God called William Tyndale for a special purpose — to translate the Scriptures into the language of the people, and to make it available for all of the people of England.

Through the work of John Wycliffe, God had been working in the hearts of the people of England for nearly 200 years. He then raised up an individual who could translate the Word of God from the original languages, Greek and Hebrew. He laid it on the heart of William Tyndale to "cause a boy that driveth a plow to know more of the Scriptures than the pope." This was a lofty goal, and one that would be reached only at great sacrifice on the part of William Tyndale.

For Reflection and Reasoning

• Review: In what language were the Scriptures originally written? From what language did John Wycliffe prepare his translation?

• Review: The people of England had been introduced to the Bible through John Wycliffe's translation, but very few individuals or families had a whole Bible.

• God gave William Tyndale a special call or burden. What was that call? Who had the Bibles? Who did Tyndale want to have the Bible?

• Who is the pope?

• Why did the leaders of England and the Roman Church not want the people to have the Bible?

Leading Idea

Though men seek to destroy the Word of God, God's Word will stand forever.

Student Text, pages 47-48

• Jeremiah 36 is an account of Jeremiah's recording the Word of God. When the words were read to the king, pages were taken from the book and cast into the fire. After the king had burned the roll, the Lord came to Jeremiah and told him to write all of the words again. "Note, Though the attempts of hell against the word of God are very daring, yet not one iota or tittle of it shall fall to the ground, nor shall the unbelief of man make the word of God of no effect. Enemies may prevail to burn many a Bible, but they cannot abolish the word of God, can neither extirpate it nor defeat the accomplishment of it. Though the tables of the law were broken, they were renewed again; and so out of the ashes of the roll that was burnt arose another Phoenix. *The word of the Lord endures for ever."*

Matthew Henry *Commentary*

• The power of God in preserving and protecting His Word can be seen in the record of William Tyndale's labor to translate the Scripture for the people.

For Reflection and Reasoning

• Jeremiah 36 contains the record of a king who did not want the Word of God to be read. He had the pages burned, but God had Jeremiah write the words again. Throughout the centuries, God protected His Word. This is evident in the life and work of Tyndale.

• Read selected verses from Jeremiah 36, perhaps verses 1, 2, 23, 27, and 28.

• Consider verses which teach us that God's Word will not be destroyed, i.e. Psalm 119:89; Isaiah 40:8; Matthew 5:18; I Peter 1:23-25.

• At the time of William Tyndale, who did not want the Word of God to be known? What did they do to people who tried to translate the Bible for the people?

• Why would the king or the church not want the people to have the Bible in their hands?

• Review the words of the song, *The Bible Stands.* Compare this song with Scriptures about the Bible being protected by God.

Cultivating Student Mastery

1. How did God protect His Word when Tyndale was taken to prison?

Leading Idea

William Tyndale, Father of the English Bible

Student Text, page 48

• "About the month of May 1524 he left London for Hamburg. . . It is not known how far the work of translation had advanced before Tyndale left for England, but at any rate the New Testament seems to have been ready for the printers by the early summer of 1525 . . .

"He was soon busily engaged on the Old Testament. In 1530 there accordingly appeared a new volume containing a translation of the Pentateuch from the original Hebrew. . . . In the spring of 1535, Tyndale was treacherously betrayed to his ever watchful enemies . . .

"Within twelve months of the martyrdom of its author at Vilvorde, the translation which 'either with glosses (marginal notes) or without' had been denounced, abused, and burnt at St. Paul's, was now, under its assumed name. . . formally approved by the King's grace, and published, . . . under the shelter of a royal proclamation and license. . ."[11]

H. W. Hoare, "The Evolution
of the English Bible"

• After Tyndale's Bible was printed in Europe, copies were secretly shipped to England. There they were sold and distributed throughout the country.

In their effort to destroy the copies of Tyndale's Bible, the authorities were seeking any copies. Merle d'Aubigne records an instance of these official efforts to destroy Tyndale's work, which were only used to further it. "Tyndale was at that time greatly embarrassed; considerable debts, incurred with his printers, compelled him to suspend his labours. Nor was this all: the prelate who had spurned him so harshly in London, had just arrived in the very city where he lay concealed . . . . What would become of him? . . . A merchant, named Augustin Packington, a clever man, but somewhat inclined to dissimulation, happening to be at Antwerp on business, hastened to pay his respects to the bishop. The latter observed, in the course of conversation: 'I should like to get hold of the books with which England is poisoned.'—'I can perhaps serve you in that matter,' replied the merchant. 'I know the Flemings, who have bought Tyndale's books; so that if your lordship will be pleased to pay for them, I will make sure of them all.'— 'Oh, oh!' thought the bishop, 'Now, as the proverb says, I shall have God by the toe. Gentle Master Packington,' he added in a flattering tone, 'I will pay for them whatsoever they cost you. I intend to burn them at St Paul's cross.' The bishop, having his hand already on Tyndale's Testaments, fancied himself on the point of seizing Tyndale himself.

"Packington, being one of those men who love to conciliate all parties, ran off to Tyndale, with whom he was intimate, and said: 'William, I know you are a poor man, and have a heap of New Testaments and books by you, for which you have beggared yourself; and I have now found a merchant who will buy them all, and with ready money too.' — 'Who is the merchant?' said Tyndale. — 'The bishop of London.' — 'Tunstall? . . . If he buys my books, it can only be to burn them.' — 'No doubt,' answered Packington; 'but what will he gain by it? The whole world will cry out against the priest who burns God's Word, and the eyes of many will be opened. Come make up your mind, William; the bishop shall have the books, you the money, and I the thanks.' . . . Tyndale resisted the proposal; Packington became more pressing. 'The question comes to this,' he said; 'shall the bishop pay for the books or shall he not? for, make up your mind . . . He will have them.' — 'I consent,' said the Reformer at last; 'I shall pay my debts, and bring out a new and more correct edition of the Testament.' The bargain was made."[12]

For Reflection and Reasoning

• Review: What does it mean to "translate" the Bible?

• Why did Tyndale have to leave England? Where did he go?

• What action did the King of England take when he learned where Tyndale was? How did Tyndale respond? Did his work on the translation of the Bible stop? Why or why not?

• The Tyndale Bibles were printed in another country and sent to England. Was the King of England happy about the Bibles being in England? What action did he take?

• Review again the verses identifying how God protects His Word.

• Use *Student Activity Pages 11-4* and

11-5. Continue timeline, *A Bible for the People.* Students cut and glue picture of Tyndale. Record: "Tyndale translated the Bible into English."

Leading Idea

Tyndale was faithful to God even in prison and in death.

Student Text, pages 48-49

• Noah Webster defines a martyr as "One who, by his death, bears witness to the truth of the gospel: Stephen was the first christian *martyr.*"

• "Friday, the 6th of October, 1536 was the day that terminated the miserable life of the reformer . . . On arriving at the scene of punishment, the reformer found a numerous crowd assembled. The government had wished to show the people the punishment of a heretic, but they only witnessed the triumph of a martyr. Tyndale was calm. 'I call God to record,' he could say, 'that I have never altered, against the voice of my conscience, one syllable of His Word. Nor would do this day, if all pleasures, honours, and riches of the earth might be given me.' The joy of hope filled his heart: yet one painful idea took possession of him. Dying far from his country, abandoned by his king, he felt saddened at the thought of that prince,

who had already persecuted so many of God's servants, and who remained obstinately rebellious against that divine light which everywhere shone around him. Tyndale would not have that soul perish through carelessness. His charity buried all the faults of the monarch: he prayed that those sins might be blotted out from before the face of God; he would have saved Henry VIII at any cost. While the executioner was fastening him to the post, the reformer exclaimed in a loud and suppliant voice: 'Lord, open the king of England's eyes!' They were his last words. Instantly afterwards he was strangled and flames consumed the martyr's body. His last cry was wafted to the British isles, and repeated in every assembly of Christians. A great death had crowned a great life."[13]

J. H. Merle d'Aubigne
The Reformation in England

For Reflection and Reasoning

• Consider the character of William Tyndale. He knew that God had called him to translate the Bible into English for the people of England. When the King of England opposed that work, did he quit? What did he do?

• Even after he was in prison, Tyndale continued his work of translating the Scripture. But, he didn't just work on the translation, he also shared the good news of the Scripture with anyone who would listen. Who were some of the people who learned of Jesus Christ through Tyndale?

• The Student Text states "he knew the Word of God was not in prison." Why was that statement true?

• Tyndale became a martyr for his faith and work on the translation of the Scriptures. What is a martyr?

• How did Tyndale's death reveal his faith in God? How did it reveal his love of England and the King of England?

Cultivating Student Mastery

1. How did Tyndale show his faithfulness to God when he was in prison?

2. When Tyndale was in prison, how did he know "the Word of God was not in prison"?

3. How did Tyndale show his trust in the Lord when he was put to death?

4. How did Tyndale show his love for England and her King?

Leading Idea

William Tyndale, Father of the English Bible

Student Text, pages 49-50

• "It has been estimated that, of Tyndale's work as above specified, our Bibles retain at the present day something like eighty per cent, in the Old Testament, and ninety per cent, in the New. If this estimate may be accepted no grander tribute could be paid to the industry, scholarship, and genius of the pioneer whose indomitable resolution enabled him to persevere in labours prolonged through twelve long years of exile from the land that in his own words he so 'loved and longed for'. with the practical certainty of a violent death staring him all the while in the face."[14]

H. W. Hoare, *The Evolution of the English Bible*

For Reflection and Reasoning

• Can the Hand of God be seen in the preservation of Tyndale's translation of the Bible?
Consider Proverbs 21:1. How was this true with King Henry VIII of England?

• What was the response of the people of England to having the Bible? What if they could not read?

• The Tyndale Bible was a very large volume, and costly for the common people of England. Did this keep them from purchasing copies? How did they overcome this challenge?

• William Tyndale's translation work was preserved in future translations — particularly the authorized King James version. This reflected the quality of Tyndale's scholarship and care in his translation. Why is William Tyndale called the "Father of the English Bible"?

• Consider the page from Tyndale's translation in the Student Text. How much of John 1 can the student read? Compare Tyndale's translation to a current translation of the Bible to see how many of the words are the same.

Suggested Student Notes

William Tyndale is the Father of the English Bible.

Cultivating Student Mastery

1. Why was William Tyndale called the "Father of the English Bible"?

Supplemental Activities

• Many historic villages include print shops which have printing presses similar to Gutenberg's press. This would make an enjoyable field trip.

• Students would also enjoy a field trip to a modern day print shop or newspaper printing plant. This would provide the opportunity to contrast the availability of printed materials in the 1500's as it differs from today. Consider: As technology improves, how is the Word of God more available to all?

CHRISTOPHER COLUMBUS
Link to the New World
3-4 Weeks

Chapter 12
Christopher Columbus
3-4 Weeks

As God was working to bring forth the *fullest expression of a Christian civilization*, Columbus was the individual prepared by God to forge the path to the New World. God uniquely prepared Columbus for the voyage spiritually, in the field of navigation, and in his own character. Columbus acknowledged the Hand of God in his *Book of Prophecies*.

"At a very early age I went to sea and have continued navigating until today. The art of sailing is favorable for anyone who wants to pursue knowledge of this world's secrets. I have already been at this business for forty years. I have sailed all the waters which, up to now, have been navigated. . . .

"At this time I have seen and put in study to look into all the Scriptures, cosmography, histories, chronicles and philosophy and other arts, which our Lord opened to my understanding (I could sense his hand upon me), so that it became clear to me that it was feasible to navigate from here to the Indies; and he unlocked within me the determination to execute the idea. And I came to your Highnesses with this ardor. All those who heard about my enterprise rejected it with laughter, scoffing at me. Neither the sciences which I mentioned above, nor the authoritative citations from them, were of any avail. In only your Highnesses remained faith and constancy. Who doubts that this illumination was from the Holy Spirit? I attest that he [the Spirit], with marvelous rays of light, consoled me through the holy and sacred Scriptures, a strong and clear testimony, . . . encouraging me to proceed, and, continually, without ceasing for a moment, they inflame me with a sense of great urgency. . . .

"I am the worst of sinners. The pity and mercy of our Lord have completely covered me whenever I have called [on him] for them. I have found the sweetest consolation in casting away all my anxiety, so as to contemplate his marvelous presence. . . .

"Your Highnesses, remember the Gospel texts and the many promises which our Savior made to us, and how all this has been put to a test: . . . The mountains will obey anyone who has faith the size of a kernel of Indian corn. All that is requested by anyone who has faith will be granted. Knock and it will be opened to you. No one should be afraid to take on any enterprise in the name of our Savior, if it is right and if the purpose is purely for his holy service . . . The working out of all things was entrusted by our Lord to each person, [but it happens] in conformity with his sovereign will, even though he gives advice to many.

"He lacks nothing that it may be in the power of men to give him. O, how good is the Lord who wishes people to perform that for which he holds himself responsible! Day and night, and at every moment, everyone should give him their most devoted thanks. . . ."[15]

• As the individual contemplates a study of Christopher Columbus from a Providential viewpoint, several questions arise which deserve consideration: Why were no efforts made for discovery of the lands to the west and establishment of permanent settlements until the late 15th century? Why, as Columbus was led by the Holy Spirit, was he drawn to the southern continent rather than the mainland of North America?

These questions were addressed by Rev. Foljambe in his sermon of 1876, "The Hand of God in American History," as he identified God's wise and beneficent timing of events as related to the discovery and preparation of America. "The discovery and preparation of this country to be the home of a great people,—the theatre of a new experiment in government, and the scene of an advancing Christian civilization,—is illustrative of this truth. Whatever may have been its prehistoric condition, for centuries it was concealed behind the mighty veil of waters from the eyes of the world. Not until the early part of the tenth century was it discovered by the Scandinavians, and only then to be hidden away again till the time should be ripe for its settlement, by a people providentially prepared for its occupancy. What a land it was, so magnificent in extent, so varied in soil and climate, so unlimited in mineral wealth and vegetable bounties; while its conformation was such as to preclude its occupants from ever being other than an united people. Harbors, and rivers, and mountain ranges link as with iron bands the far separated localities. Yet all this thorough preparation by which this continent had been builded and furnished, was not available until God's hour had come for its occupancy . . . When he had created a stalwart race, and ordained them for the settlement of his country, and for laying the foundations of a higher civilization than the world had yet seen, and when they had started on their mission of light, and freedom, and religion, then he suddenly dropped the veil from this continent, and there arose before the astonished vision of the nations the splendors of the Western World."[16]

> **Leading Idea**
>
> # God prepares men and then He causes events.
>
> Student Text, page 51

• As the history of liberty is studied, the evidence is clear that the Bible in the hands of the people is causative to the establishment of Christian civil government. The door to the New World could only be opened when a people were prepared to plant on this soil a Christian form of civil government. Historian Verna Hall elucidated this truth for consideration: "Almost immediately following Wycliffe's translation of the whole Bible, God began to call forth men to develop the many scientific and economic fields which would be necessary to enable man to sail the seas, explore, and finally settle the lands across the vast Atlantic ocean. With the correlation so plain and easily documented between the Bible being made available to the individual in England, and the almost sudden development of basic inventions necessary for sailing the seas, and colonizing America, it is strange this is not better known by American Christians who have so dramatically benefitted thereby. God had been reserving the land we know as the original thirteen colonies to begin establishing the Christian form of civil government, until there could be a handful of 'peculiar people' properly rooted and grounded in His Word."[17]

• ". . . As far as authenticated history extends, nothing was known of terra firma, and the islands of the western hemisphere, until their discovery toward the close of the fifteenth century. A wandering bark may occasionally have lost sight of the landmarks of the old continents, and been driven by tempests across the wilderness of waters long before the invention of the compass, but never returned to reveal the secrets of the ocean. And though, from time to time, some document has floated to the shores of the old world, giving its wondering inhabi-

tants evidences of land far beyond their watery horizon; yet no one ventured to spread a sail, and seek that land enveloped in mystery and peril. Or if the legends of the Scandinavian voyagers be correct . . . they had but transient glimpses of the new world, leading to no certain or permanent knowledge, and in a little time lost again to mankind. Certain it is that at the beginning of the fifteenth century, when the most intelligent minds were seeking in every direction for the scattered lights of geographical knowledge, a profound ignorance prevailed among the learned as to the western regions of the Atlantic; its vast waters were regarded with awe and wonder, seeming to bound the world as with a chaos, into which conjecture could not penetrate, and enterprise feared to adventure. . ."

Washington Irving, *The Life and Voyages of Christopher Columbus*

For Reflection and Reasoning

• Review: When did Wycliffe translate the Bible? In what language was it translated? How did the people learn about the Bible? How many people in England knew about the Bible? See Student Text, pages 42-44.

• Look at a globe or world map. Identify the continents. At the time of Christopher Columbus, which continents were known by the people in England and Europe?

• Introduce the idea of the Old World and

the New World.

• Review: What is a link? Who was the link to the New World?

• See *Student Activity Page 12-1*. The poem, *To* _____, was written to a young girl as the introduction to a biography of Columbus. To whet the student's appetite for the many adventures found in the text, this poem could be read with the students before they begin their study. The student will enjoy writing his name on the line and coloring the picture of Columbus.

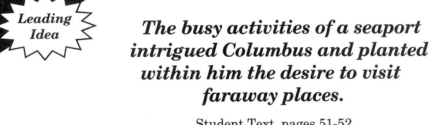

Leading Idea

The busy activities of a seaport intrigued Columbus and planted within him the desire to visit faraway places.

Student Text, pages 51-52

• Washington Irving's historic writings include the lives of both Christopher Co-

lumbus and George Washington, for whom he had been named. At the age of five he had been presented to Washington and was later inspired by the childhood memory to write about the Father of Our Country. . . . The objective of *The Life and Voyages of Christopher Columbus* was "to relate the deeds and fortunes of the mariner who first had the judgment to divine, and the intrepidity to brave the mysteries of this perilous deep; and who, by his hardy genius, his inflexible constancy, and his heroic courage, brought the ends of the earth into communication with each other. The narrative of his troubled life is the link which connects the history of the old world with that of the new."[18]

The Life and Voyages of Christopher Columbus remains a leading, authentic resource based on original source documents. His insights assist the reader in discerning how greatly the discovery rested upon the direction of Providence, the monumental character of Columbus, and the Biblical ideas of men and nations on which the American republic was founded. To assist the teacher, selections have been included throughout the study on Christopher Columbus.

• "Christopher Columbus, or Columbo, as the name is written in Italian, was born in the city of Genoa, about the year 1435. [Modern scholars date Columbus's birth at 1450.] He was the son of Dominico Columbo, a wool comber, and Susannah Fontanarossa, his wife, and it would seem that his ancestors had followed the same handicraft for several generations in Genoa. . . .

"Columbus was the oldest of four children; having two brothers, Bartholomew and Giacomo, or James (written Diego in Spanish), and one sister, of whom nothing is known but that she was married to a person in obscure life called Giacomo Bavarello. At a very early age Columbus evinced a decided inclination for the sea; his education, therefore, was mainly directed to fit him for maritime life, but was as general as the narrow means of his father would permit. Besides the ordinary branches of reading, writing, grammar and arithmetic, he was instructed in the Latin tongue, and made some proficiency in drawing and design. For a short time, also, he was sent to the university of Pavia, where he studied geometry, geography, astronomy and navigation. . . . according to his own account he entered upon a nautical life when but fourteen years of age.

"In tracing the early history of a man like Columbus, whose actions have had a vast effect on human affairs, it is interesting to notice how much has been owing to external influences, how much to an inborn propensity of the genius. . . .

"The nautical propensity, however, evinced by Columbus in early life, is common to boys of enterprising spirit and lively imagination brought up in maritime cities; to whom the sea is the high road to adventure and the region of romance. Genoa, too, walled in and straitened on the land side by rugged mountains, yielded but little scope for enterprise on the shore, while an opulent and widely extended commerce, visiting every country, and a roving marine, battling in every sea, naturally led forth her children upon the waves, as their propitious element. . . ."

Washington Irving, *The Life and Voyages of Christopher Columbus*

For Reflection and Reasoning

• How did Genoa influence Columbus's chosen occupation and prepare him to fulfill it?

• Consider the picture of Columbus in the Student Text, page 51. What would Columbus have seen as he looked out into the harbor?

• Who arranged Columbus's life so that these influences could be in place? Why?

• Columbus spent much time learning. What is the same as the things you are learning? What is different?

• Locate the country of Italy, the city of Genoa, and the surrounding waterways on a map. Where did Columbus sail?

• See *Student Activity Page 12-2.* Begin a map of Europe. Label Italy as the birthplace of Columbus.

• Find enjoyable songs about sailing for the children to learn. These can be sung periodically throughout the study of Christopher Columbus.

Suggested Student Notes

Columbus was born near the Mediterranean Sea.

Leading Idea

God created Columbus with the unique interests, spirit, and abilities to be a sailor.

• "The strong passion for geographical knowledge, also, felt by Columbus in early life, and which inspired his after career, was incident to the age in which he lived. Geographical discovery was the brilliant path of light which was forever to distinguish the fifteenth century. . . .

"The knowledge thus reviving was limited and imperfect; yet, like the return of the morning light, it seemed to call a new creation into existence, and broke, with all the charm of wonder, upon imaginative minds. . . .

"Such was the state of information and feeling with respect to this interesting science, in the early part of the fifteenth century. An interest still more intense was awakened by the discoveries which began to be made along the Atlantic coasts of Africa; and must have been particularly felt among a maritime and commercial people like the Genoese. To these circumstances may we ascribe the enthusiastic devotion which Columbus imbibed in his childhood for cosmographical studies, and which influenced all his after fortunes.

"The short time passed by him at the university of Pavia was barely sufficient to give him the rudiments of the necessary sciences; the familiar acquaintance with them, which he evinced in after life, must have been the result of diligent self-schooling, in casual hours of study amid the cares and vicissitudes of a rugged and wandering life. He was one of those men of strong natural genius, who, from having to contend at their very outset with privations and impediments, acquire an intrepidity in encountering and a facility in vanquishing difficulties, throughout their career. Such men learn to effect great purposes with small means, supplying this deficiency by the resources of their own energy and invention. This, from his earliest commencement, throughout the whole of his life, was one of the remarkable features in the history of Columbus. In every undertaking, the scantiness and apparent insufficiency of his means enhance the grandeur of his achievements."

Washington Irving, *The Life and Voyages of Christopher Columbus*

For Reflection and Reasoning

• In order to be a leader, a person must have goals and dreams. What dream did Columbus have?

• To accomplish his goals, Columbus needed certain character qualities. What were they?

• What is the character needed to be a good sailor?

• Identify the ways in which sailing is controlled by the weather.

• Continue outlining and labeling the map of Europe. Label the Mediterranean Sea.

In some of his darkest and most difficult hours, God was bringing Columbus to exactly the right place.

Student Text, pages 52-53

• "The seafaring life of the Mediterranean in those days was hazardous and daring. A commercial expedition resembled a warlike cruise, and the maritime merchant had often to fight his way from port to port. . . .

"Such was the rugged school in which Columbus was reared, and it would have been deeply interesting to have marked the early development of his genius amid its stern adversities. All this instructive era of his history, however, is covered with darkness. . . .

". . . A desperate engagement took place; the vessels grappled each other, and the crews fought hand to hand, and from ship to ship. The battle lasted from morning until evening, with great carnage on both sides. The vessel commanded by Columbus was engaged with a huge Venetian galley. They threw hand grenades and other fiery missiles, and the galley was wrapped in flames. The vessels were fastened together by chains and grappling irons, and could not be separated; both were involved in one conflagration, and soon became a mere blazing mass. The crews threw themselves into the sea; Columbus seized an oar, which was floating within reach, and being an expert swimmer, attained the shore, though full two leagues distant. It pleased God, says his son Fernando, to give him strength, that he might preserve him for greater things. After recovering from his exhaustion he repaired to Lisbon, where he found many of his Genoese countrymen, and was induced to take up his residence. . . ."

Washington Irving, *The Life and Voyages of Christopher Columbus*

For Reflection and Reasoning

• Review: What is Providence?

• Why did it please God to preserve Columbus's life? Why did God send Columbus to Portugal?

• What qualities of character enabled Columbus to swim for many hours during the night until he finally reached shore? As a class, write a sentence identifying Columbus's character evidenced in his arrival in Portugal. Students may record the sentence in their notebooks.

• Continue outlining and labeling the map of Europe. Label Portugal.

• Sing songs about God's protection.

How do we reach the Indies?

Student Text, pages 53-54

• "The career of modern discovery had commenced shortly before the time of Columbus, and at the period of which we are treating was prosecuted with great activity by Portugal. . . .

"The grand impulse to discovery was not given by chance, but was the deeply meditated effort of one master mind. This was Prince Henry of Portugal . . .

"It was the grand idea of Prince Henry, by circumnavigating Africa to open a direct and easy route to the source of this commerce, to turn it in a golden tide upon his country. He was, however, before the age in thought, and had to counteract ignorance and prejudice, and to endure the delays to which vivid and penetrating minds are subjected, from the tardy cooperations of the dull and the doubtful. . . .

"To dispel these errors, and to give a scope to navigation equal to the grandeur of his designs, Prince Henry established a naval college, and erected an observatory at Sagres, and he invited thither the most eminent professors of the nautical faculties; . . .

"The effects of this establishment were soon apparent. All that was known relative to geography and navigation was gathered together and reduced to system. A vast improvement took place in maps. The compass was also brought into more general use, especially among the Portuguese, rendering the mariner more bold and venturous, by enabling him to navigate in the most gloomy day and in the darkest night. . . .

"Henry died . . . without accomplishing the great object of his ambition. . . . The discoveries of the Portuguese were the wonder and admiration of the fifteenth century, and Portugal, from being one of the least among nations, suddenly rose to be one of the most important.

"All this was effected, not by arms, but by arts; not by the stratagems of a cabinet, but by the wisdom of a college. . . .

"Henry, at his death, left it in charge to his country to prosecute the route to India . . .The fame of the Portuguese discoveries, and of the expeditions continually setting out, drew the attention of the world. Strangers from all parts, the learned, the curious, and the adventurous, resorted to Lisbon to inquire into the particulars or to participate in the advantages of these enterprises. Among these was Christopher Columbus . . ."

Washington Irving, *The Life and Voyages of Christopher Columbus*

For Reflection and Reasoning

• Bring samples of spices to class for the students to observe the great variety of tastes and smells. Help them understand how spices make food taste better, and why the Europeans wanted them. It might be interesting to bring the spices that are pictured in the student text. Also, identify how spices help to keep food from spoiling.

• Look at a globe or map to identify the countries of India, China, and Cipango. Cipango is the modern country of Japan. Consider the route the caravans may have taken across the mountains and deserts of Asia to arrive at the Mediterranean Sea.

• What is a seaport? On the map, locate seaports along the coast of Asia and seaports of Europe.

• On the map, or globe, identify the route which Prince Henry proposed for reaching the Indies. Why would his plan have been easier than the route of the caravans?

Cultivating Student Mastery

1. What did the sailors learn in Prince Henry's school?

2. How did the compass help the sailors?

Leading Idea

God brought Columbus to Portugal for a special reason.

Student Text, page 55

• "Columbus arrived at Lisbon about the year 1470. He was at that time in the full vigor of manhood, and of an engaging presence. Minute descriptions are given of his person. . .tall, well-formed, muscular, and of an elevated and dignified demeanor. His visage was long, and neither full nor meagre; his complexion fair and freckled, and inclined to ruddy; his nose aquiline; his cheek-bones were rather high, his eyes light gray, and apt to kindle; his whole countenance had an air of authority. His hair, in his youthful days, was of a light color; but care and trouble, . . . soon turned it gray, and at thirty years of age it was quite white. He was moderate and simple in diet and apparel, eloquent in discourse, engaging and affable with strangers, and his amiableness and suavity in domestic life strongly attached his household to his person. His temper was naturally irritable; but he subdued it by the magnanimity of his spirit, comporting himself with a courteous and gentle gravity, and never indulging in any intemperance of language. Throughout his life he was noted for strict attention to the offices of religion, observing rigorously the fasts and ceremonies of the church; nor did his piety consist in mere forms, but partook of that lofty and solemn enthusiasm with which his whole character was strongly tinctured.

"While at Lisbon, he was accustomed to attend religious service at the chapel of the convent of All Saints. In this convent were certain ladies of rank . . . With one of these Columbus became acquainted. . . . The acquaintance soon ripened into attachment, and ended in marriage. . . .

"The newly married couple resided with the mother of the bride. The latter, perceiving the interest which Columbus took in all matters concerning the sea, related to him all she knew of the voyages and expeditions of her late husband, and brought him all his papers, charts, journals, and memorandums. In this way he became acquainted with the routes of the Portuguese, . . . When on shore, he supported his family by making maps and charts. His narrow circumstances obliged him to observe a strict economy; yet we are told that he appropriated a part of his scanty means to the succor of his aged father at Genoa, and to the education of his younger brothers. . . .

"While his geographical labors thus elevated him to a communication with the learned, they were peculiarly calculated to foster a train of thoughts favorable to nautical enterprise. From constantly comparing maps and charts, and noting the progress and direction of discovery, he was led to perceive how much of the world remained unknown, and to meditate on the means of exploring it. . . ."

Washington Irving, *The Life and Voyages of Christopher Columbus*

For Reflection and Reasoning

• Review: How had Columbus arrived in Portugal?

• Locate Lisbon on the map.

• Why was it important for Columbus to be in Portugal? How did it help to prepare him for his future voyage? What knowledge of sailing could be found in Portugal that was not found anywhere else in the world?

- How was the lady whom Columbus married a special blessing to Columbus? Consider his personal life. Also consider his future voyages to the New World.

- What did Columbus learn from the maps and charts?

Leading Idea

Columbus believed God wanted him to sail west to the Indies

Student Text, pages 55-56

- ". . . The earth was a terraqueous sphere or globe, which might be travelled round from east to west, and that men stood foot to foot when on opposite points. The circumference from east to west, at the equator, Columbus divided . . . into twenty-four hours of fifteen degrees each, making three hundred and sixty degrees. Of these he imagined . . . that fifteen hours had been known to the ancients . . . The Portuguese had advanced the western frontier one hour more by the discovery of the Azores and Cape de Verde Islands. There remained, then, according to the estimation of Columbus, eight hours, or one third of the circumference of the earth, unknown and unexplored. . . . Granting these premises, it was manifest that, by pursuing a direct course from east to west, a navigator would arrive at the extremity of Asia, and discover any intervening land.

". . . writings had weight in convincing him that the intervening ocean could be but of moderate expanse, and easy to be traversed. . . .

"In corroboration of the idea that Asia, or, as he always terms it India, stretched far to the east, so as to occupy the greater part of the unexplored space, the narratives are cited of Marco Polo and John Mandeville. These travellers had visited, in the thirteenth and fourteenth centuries, the remote parts of Asia, far beyond the regions laid down by Ptolemy; and their accounts of the extent of that continent to the eastward had a great effect in convincing Columbus that a voyage to the west, of no long duration, would bring him to its shores, or to the extensive and wealthy islands which lie adjacent. . . .

"It is singular how much the success of this great undertaking depended upon two happy errors, the imaginary extent of Asia to the east, and the supposed smallness of the earth, both errors of the most learned and profound philosophers, but without which Columbus would hardly have ventured upon his enterprise. . . ."

Washington Irving, *The Life and Voyages of Christopher Columbus*

For Reflection and Reasoning

- What was Columbus's plan for sailing to the Indies? How was his plan different than that of Prince Henry?

- Using a globe, compare the route which Columbus proposed to the route which Prince Henry had proposed.

- Why did Columbus think his route would be easier than traveling across

mountains and deserts? Why did he think it would be easier than Prince Henry's plan?

- Man's knowledge of the earth has expanded over the centuries. Not long before Columbus, men thought the earth was flat. If men were depending simply on what they could see, why would they have thought the earth was flat?

- By the time of Columbus, men knew

that the earth was round. What wrong ideas did they have? How many continents did they think there were?

• Men thought the Atlantic Ocean was not large. How would that affect Columbus's voyage?

• Why was it good that Columbus did not know how big the earth was?

• See *Student Activity Page 12-3*. Reason from the Student Text to complete the chart, identifying Prince Henry's and Columbus's plans for reaching the Indies.

Cultivating Student Mastery

1. Why did Columbus think his plan was the best?

Sailing to the Indies

Prince Henry's Plan	Columbus's Plan
Sail around Africa	Sail across the Atlantic Ocean

Leading Idea

In spite of difficulties, Columbus did not give up.

Student Text, pages 56-57

• "Discovery advanced slowly along the coasts of Africa, and the mariners feared to cruise far into the southern hemisphere, with the stars of which they were totally unacquainted. . . .

"The time, however, was at hand, that was to extend the sphere of navigation. The era was propitious to the quick advancement of knowledge. . . .

"The African discoveries had conferred great glory upon Portugal . . . The project of Prince Henry, which had now been tardily prosecuted for half a century, had excited a curiosity about the remote parts of Asia, and revived all the accounts, true and fabulous, of travellers. . . .

". . . John II. partook largely of the popular excitement produced by these narrations. . . . The magnificent idea he had formed of the remote parts of the East made him extremely anxious that the splendid project of Prince Henry should be realized, and the Portuguese

flag penetrate to the Indian seas. Impatient of the slowness with which his discoveries advanced along the coast of Africa, and of the impediments which every cape and promontory presented to nautical enterprise, he called in the aid of science to devise some means by which greater scope and certainty might be given to navigation. . . . The result of their conferences and labors was the application of the astrolabe to navigation, enabling the seaman, by the altitude of the sun, to ascertain his distance from the equator. This instrument has since been improved and modified into the modern quadrant, of which, even at its first introduction, it possessed all the essential advantages.

"It is impossible to describe the effect produced upon navigation by this invention. It cast it loose at once from its long bondage to the land, and set it free to rove the deep. The mariner now, instead of coasting the shores like the ancient navigators, and, if driven from the land, groping his way back in doubt and apprehension by the uncertain guidance of the stars, might adventure boldly into unknown seas, confident of being able to trace his course by means of the compass and the astrolabe. . . ."

Washington Irving, *The Life and Voyages of Christopher Columbus*

For Reflection and Reasoning

• Review: What was Columbus's plan for finding the Indies?

• Columbus had a plan, but what did he not have? He needed help to make his plan work.

• Why did Columbus think the King of Portugal might want to help him? Did he want to find a route to the Indies? Why did he not want to help?

• Was Columbus discouraged? Would it have been easy for Columbus to become discouraged? Why did Columbus not give up?

• Read the poem aloud, "Don't Give Up".

What character quality does this poem identify? How did Columbus's life demonstrate the character identified in the poem?

Don't Give Up
Phoebe Carey

If you tried and have not won,
  Never stop for crying:
All that's great and good is done
  Just by patient trying. . .

Cultivating Student Mastery

1. When the King of Portugal did not help Columbus, what did Columbus do?

Leading Idea

Columbus was Providentially directed to the individuals best suited to promote his cause.

Student Text, pages 57-58

• "The time when Columbus thus sought his fortunes at the court of Spain coincided with one of the most brilliant periods of the Spanish monarchy. . . .

"Ferdinand was of the middle stature, well proportioned, and hardy and active from athletic exercise. His carriage was free, erect, and majestic. He had a clear, serene forehead, which appeared more lofty from his head being partly bald. His eyebrows were large and parted, and, like his hair, of a bright chestnut; his eyes were clear and animated; his complexion was somewhat ruddy, and scorched by the toils of war; his mouth moderate, well formed, and

gracious in its expression; his teeth white, though small and irregular; his voice sharp; his speech quick and fluent. His genius was clear and comprehensive, his judgment grave and certain. He was simple in dress and diet, equable in his temper, devout in his religion and so indefatigable in business, that it was said he seemed to repose himself by working. He was a great observer and judge of men, and unparalleled in the science of the cabinet. Such is the picture given him by the Spanish historians of his time. It has been added, however, that he had more of bigotry than religion; that his ambition was craving rather than magnanimous; that he made war less like a paladin than a prince, less for glory than for mere dominion; and that his policy was cold, selfish, and artful. . . .

"Contemporary writers have been enthusiastic in their descriptions of Isabella, but time has sanctioned their eulogies. She is one of the purest and most beautiful characters in the pages of history. She was well formed, of the middle size, with great dignity and gracefulness of deportment, and a mingled gravity and sweetness of demeanor. Her complexion was fair; her hair auburn, inclining to red; her eyes were of a clear blue, with a benign expression, and there was a singular modesty in her countenance, gracing, as it did, a wonderful firmness of purpose and earnestness of spirit. Though strongly attached to her husband and studious of his fame, yet she always maintained her distinct rights as an allied prince. She exceeded him in beauty, in personal dignity, in acuteness of genius, and in grandeur of soul. Combining the active and resolute qualities of man with the softer charities of woman, she mingled in the warlike councils of her husband, engaged personally in his enterprises, and in some instances surpassed him in the firmness and intrepidity of her measures; while, being inspired with a truer idea of glory, she infused a more lofty and generous temper into his subtle and calculating policy.

"It is in the civil history of their reign, however, that the character of Isabella shines most illustrious. Her fostering and maternal care was continually directed to reform the laws, and heal the ills engendered by a long course of internal wars. She loved her people, and while diligently seeking their good, she mitigated, as much as possible, the harsh measures of her husband, directed to the same end, but inflamed by a mistaken zeal. . . . While all her public thoughts and acts were princely and august, her private habits were simple, frugal, and unostentatious. In the intervals of state business she assembled round her the ablest men in literature and science, and directed herself by their counsels, in promoting letters and arts. . . . She promoted the distribution of honors and rewards for the promulgation of knowledge; she fostered the art of printing recently invented, and encouraged the establishment of presses in every part of the kingdom; . . .

". . . Columbus appeared in the royal presence with modesty, yet self-possession, neither dazzled nor daunted by the splendor of the court or the awful majesty of the throne. He unfolded his plan with eloquence and zeal, for he felt himself, as he afterward declared, kindled as with a fire from on high, and considered himself the agent chosen by Heaven to accomplish its grand designs.

"Ferdinand was too keen a judge of men not to appreciate the character of Columbus. He perceived that, however soaring might be his imagination, and vast and visionary his views, his whole scheme had scientific and practical foundation. . . .

"When Columbus took his stand before this learned body, he had appeared the plain and simple navigator; somewhat daunted, perhaps, by the greatness of his task and the august nature of his auditory. But he had a degree of religious feeling which gave him a confidence in the execution of what he conceived his great errand, and he was of an ardent temperament that became heated in action by its own generous fires. . . . "

Washington Irving, *The Life and Voyages of Christopher Columbus*

For Reflection and Reasoning

• Review the location of Portugal.

• Locate the country of Spain on a globe or map.

• How might Columbus and Diego have traveled from Portugal to Spain? How long might it have taken to make the journey? Why did Columbus not give up?

• Columbus was Providentially directed

to the appropriate individuals who would take an interest in his cause. Who promised to help?

• How did the King and Queen hear about Columbus's plan? Why did they not help Columbus?

• How long did Columbus wait in Spain? What did other people think of Columbus's plan? Besides the duke, who else thought the King and Queen would help Columbus?

• Continue outlining and labeling the map of Europe. Label Spain.

• *Student Activity Page 12-4.* Students may color the banner design. Or, *Student Activity Page 12-5.* Cut and glue the banners onto a piece of colored paper.

Leading Idea

Columbus waited many years, and suffered poverty and disappointment; but in God's perfect time, friends were raised up to help him along the path to success.

Student Text, pages 59-60

• Columbus welcomed the termination of Spain's campaign against the Moors, hoping to at last receive a decision about his proposed enterprise. But he was again disappointed.

"If the bustle and turmoil of this campaign prevented the intended conference, the concerns of Columbus fared no better during the subsequent rejoicings. Ferdinand and Isabella entered Seville in February, 1490, with great pomp and triumph. There were then preparations made for the marriage of their eldest daughter, the Princess Isabella, with the Prince Don Alonzo, heir apparent of Portugal. . . . Throughout the whole winter and spring the court was in a continual tumult of parade and pleasure, and nothing was to be seen at Seville but feasts, tournaments, and torchlight processions. What chance had Columbus of being heard amid these alternate uproars of war and festivity? . . .

"During all this time he was exposed to continual scoffs and indignities, being ridiculed by the light and ignorant as a mere dreamer, and stigmatized by the illiberal as an adventurer. The very chil-

dren, it is said, pointed to their foreheads as he passed, being taught to regard him as a kind of madman. . . .

"He was wearied, if not incensed, at the repeated postponements he had experienced by which several years had been consumed. . . . Renouncing all further confidence, therefore, in vague promises, which had so often led to disappointment, and giving up all hopes of countenance from the throne, he turned his back upon Seville, indignant at the thoughts of having been beguiled out of so many precious years of waning existence.

"About half a league from the little seaport of Palos de Moguer in Andalusia there stood . . . an ancient convent of Franciscan friars dedicated to Santa Maria de Rabida. One day a stranger on foot, in humble guise but of a distinguished air, accompanied by a small boy, stopped at the gate of the convent and asked of the porter a little bread and water for his child. While receiving this humble refreshment, the prior of the convent, Juan Perez de Marchena, happening to pass by, was struck with the appearance of the stranger, and observing from his air and accent that he was a foreigner, entered into conversation with him, and soon learned the particulars of his story. That stranger was Columbus.

". . . [The prior] was greatly interested by the conversation of Columbus, and struck with the grandeur of his views. . . .

"When he found, however, that the voyager was on the point of abandoning Spain to seek patronage in the court of France and that so important an enterprise was about to be lost forever to the country, the patriotism of the good friar took alarm. He detained Columbus as his guest, and, diffident of his own judgment, sent for a scientific friend to converse with him. . . . several conferences took place at the convent, at which several of the veteran mariners of Palos were present. Among these was Martin Alonzo Pinzon, the head of a family of wealthy and experienced navigators of the place, celebrated for their adventurous expeditions. . . .

"Friar Juan Perez was confirmed in his faith by the concurrence of those learned and practical councillors. He had once been confessor to the queen, and knew she was always accessible to persons of his sacred calling. He proposed to write to her immediately on the subject, and entreated Columbus to delay his journey until an answer could be received. The latter was easily persuaded, for he felt as if, in leaving Spain, he was again abandoning his home. . . .

"Isabella had always been favorably disposed to the proposition of Columbus. She wrote in reply to Juan Perez, thanking him for his timely services, and requesting that he would repair immediately to the court, leaving Christopher Columbus in confident hope until he should hear further from her. . . .

"The queen requested that Columbus might be again sent to her, and, with the kind considerateness which characterized her, bethinking herself of his poverty, and his humble plight, ordered that twenty thousand maravedies in florins should be forwarded to him, to bear his travelling expenses, to provide him with a mule for his journey, and to furnish him with decent raiment, that he might make a respectable appearance at the court. . . .

Washington Irving, *The Life and Voyages of Christopher Columbus*

For Reflection and Reasoning

• How was Columbus Providentially directed to the appropriate individuals who would take an interest in his cause?

• How was Columbus able to remain true to his ideas when the opposition was so strong?

• Contrast decision-making by whim and decision-making by principle. Give evidence of the method Columbus used.

• Columbus felt the full responsibility for seeing his plan become a reality. How did this influence his actions?

• How had Friar Perez been Providentially prepared to meet a need in Columbus's life and vision? Define patriotism and Biblically research its ideas. How did the friar's patriotism govern his actions and benefit his country?

How do these events prove that one individual can dramatically change the course of history?

• See *Student Activity Page 12-6*. Read and discuss the poem, *Columbus at the Convent*.

Cultivating Student Mastery

1. On two different occasions Columbus was ready to leave Spain. How did God keep him from leaving each time?

> **Leading Idea**
>
> ## *"The King's Heart is in the hand of the Lord." Proverbs 21:1*
>
> Student Text, pages 60-62

• "It is impossible not to admire the great constancy of purpose and loftiness of spirit displayed by Columbus, ever since he had conceived the sublime idea of his discovery. More than eighteen years had elapsed since his correspondence with Paulo Toscanelli of Florence, wherein he had announced his design. The greatest part of that time had been consumed in applications at various courts. During that period, what poverty, neglect, ridicule, contumely, and disappointment had he not suffered! Nothing, however, could shake his perseverance, nor make him descend to terms which he considered beneath the dignity of his enterprise. In all his negotiations he forgot his present obscurity; he forgot his present indigence; his ardent imagination realized the magnitude of his contemplated discoveries, and he felt himself negotiating about empire. . . .

". . . With an enthusiasm worthy of herself and of the cause, Isabella exclaimed 'I undertake the enterprise for my own crown of Castile, and will pledge my jewels to raise the necessary funds.' This was the proudest moment in the life of Isabella; it stamped her renown forever as the patroness of the discovery of the New World. . ."

Washington Irving, *The Life and Voyages of Christopher Columbus*

For Reflection and Reasoning

• Who controls the king? See Teacher's Guide, pages 47-48.

• How is character defined? How is it formed in the life of the individual?

What influences had operated in Columbus's life to produce his character? How did his own personal character determine the outcome of his plans for sailing to the Indies?

• What qualities of Columbus's character caused the King and Queen to respect his ideas?

• How does this event illustrate the truth of Proverbs 21:1?

• Columbus had invested vast amounts of time and effort into achieving his goal to cross the Atlantic to reach the Indies. How did the terms of this agreement remunerate him for his efforts?

Cultivating Student Mastery

1. Why did Columbus deserve to be rewarded if his voyage succeeded?

2. How do you know the Queen wanted very much to help Columbus?

Leading Idea

In God's perfect time, friends were raised up to help him along the path to success.

Student Text, pages 62-63

• ". . . a royal order was read by a notary public, commanding the authorities of Palos to have two caravels ready for sea within ten days . . . and to place them and their crews at the disposal of Columbus. . . .

"With these orders the authorities promised implicit compliance; but when the nature of the intended expedition came to be known, astonishment and dismay fell upon the little community. The ships and crews demanded for such a desperate service were regarded in the light of sacrifices. The owners of vessels refused to furnish them; the boldest seamen shrank from such a wild and chimerical cruise into the wilderness of the ocean. . . .

"Weeks elapsed without a vessel being procured, or anything else being done in fulfilment of the royal orders. . . . At length Martin Alonzo Pinzon stepped forward, with his brother Vicente Yañez Pinzon, both navigators of great courage and ability, owners of vessels, and having seamen in their employ. . . . They engaged to sail on the expedition, and furnished one of the vessels required. Others, with their owners and crews, were pressed into the service by the magistrates under the arbitrary mandate of the sovereigns; and it is a striking instance of the despotic authority exercised over commerce in those times, that respectable individuals should thus be compelled to engage, with persons and ships, in what appeared to them a mad and desperate enterprise. During the equipment of the vessels, troubles and difficulties

arose among the seamen who had been compelled to embark. . . . All kinds of obstacles were thrown in the way . . . to retard or defeat the voyage. The calkers employed upon the vessels did their work in a careless and imperfect manner, and on being commanded to do it over again absconded. Some of the seamen who had enlisted willingly repented of their hardihood, or were dissuaded by their relatives, and sought to retract; others deserted and concealed themselves. Everything had to be effected by the most harsh and arbitrary measures, and in defiance of popular prejudice and opposition.

"The influence and example of the Pinzons had a great effect in allaying this opposition, and inducing many of their friends and relatives to embark. . . .

"After the great difficulties made by various courts in patronizing this enterprise, it is surprising how inconsiderable armament was required. It is evident that Columbus had reduced his requisitions to the narrowest limits . . . The smallness of the vessels was considered an advantage by Columbus, in a voyage of discovery, enabling him to run close to the shores, and to enter shallow rivers and harbors. . . . But that such long and perilous expeditions, into unknown seas, should be undertaken in vessels without decks, and that they should live through the violent tempests, by which they were frequently assailed, remain among the singular circumstances of these daring voyages. . . ."

Washington Irving, *The Life and Voyages of Christopher Columbus*

For Reflection and Reasoning

• How were the remaining obstacles to the voyage Providentially overcome?

• The King and Queen ordered that ships should be made ready. They also ordered that crews should be made available to Columbus. If the men were not willing to make the voyage, how would this affect their attitude? Why were they afraid?

How did it affect Columbus's effort? Why would it be better if the sailors had wanted to make the voyage?

• List the many preparations which had to be made before Columbus and his fleet could sail. This could be a class activity or individual student project.

• Students may draw a picture of the three ships.

Leading Idea

The great adventure began.

Student Text, pages 63-64

• "It was on Friday, the 3d of August, 1492, early in the morning, that Columbus set sail . . . steering in a southwesterly direction for the Canary Islands, whence it was his intention to strike due west. As a guide by which to sail, he had prepared a map or chart, . . . It exhibits the coasts of Europe and Africa from the south of Ireland to the end of Guinea, and opposite to them, on the other side of the Atlantic, the extremity of Asia, or, as it was termed, India. Between them is placed the island of Cipango, or Japan, which, according to Marco Polo, lay fifteen hundred miles distant from the Asiatic coast. In his computations Columbus advanced this island about a thousand leagues too much to the east, supposing it to be about the situation of Florida; and at this island he hoped first to arrive.

"The exultation of Columbus at finding himself, after so many years of baffled hope, fairly launched on his grand enterprise, was checked by his want of confidence in the resolution and perseverance of his crews. As long as he remained within reach of Europe, there was no security that, in a moment of repentance and alarm, they might not renounce the prosecution of the voyage, and insist on a return. Symptoms soon ap-

peared to warrant his apprehensions. On the third day the Pinta made signal of distress; her rudder was discovered to be broken and unhung. This Columbus surmised to be done through the contrivance of the owners of the caravel, Gomez Rascon and Christoval Quintero, to disable their vessel, and cause her to be left behind. As has already been observed, they had been pressed into the service greatly against their will, and their caravel seized upon for the expedition, in conformity to the royal orders.

"Columbus was much disturbed at this occurrence. It gave him a foretaste of further difficulties to be apprehended from crews partly enlisted on compulsion, and all full of doubt and foreboding. Trivial obstacles might, in the present critical state of his voyage, spread panic and mutiny through his ships, and entirely defeat the expedition.

"The wind was blowing strongly at the time, so that he could not render assistance without endangering his own vessel. Fortunately, Martin Alonzo Pinzon commanded the Pinta, and being an adroit and able seaman, succeeded in securing the rudder with cords, so as to bring the vessel into management. This, however, was but a temporary and inadequate expedient; the fastenings gave way again on the following day, and the other ships were obliged to shorten sail until the rudder could be secured.

"This damaged state of the Pinta, as well as her being in a leaky condition, determined the admiral to touch at the Canary Islands, and seek a vessel to replace her.

"They were detained upward of three weeks among these islands, seeking in vain another vessel. They were obliged, therefore, to make a new rudder for the Pinta, and repair her for the voyage. The latine sails of the Nina were also altered into square sails, that she might work more steadily and securely, and be able to keep company with the other vessels. . . ."

Washington Irving, *The Life and Voyages of Christopher Columbus*

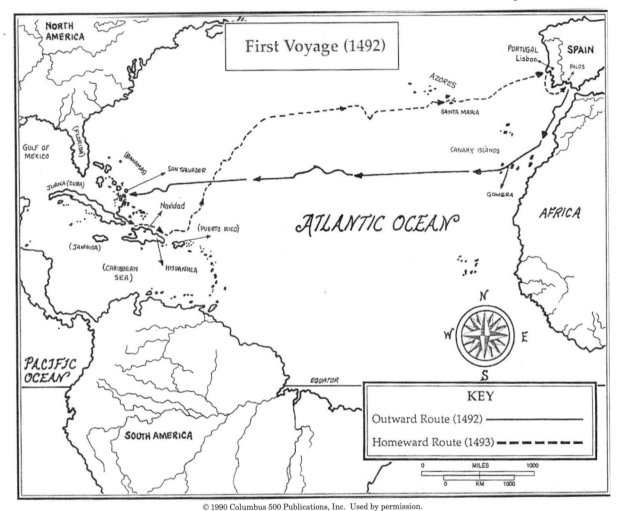

© 1990 Columbus 500 Publications, Inc. Used by permission.

For Reflection and Reasoning

• When the ships departed from Spain, they left from the port at Palos. Locate Palos on a map.

• How can Providential protection be seen in the situation with the Pinta's broken rudder?

• The first stop on their voyage was in the Canary Islands. Locate the Canary Islands on a map.

• Voluntary consent is the basis on which American enterprise and government is established. How did Columbus suffer because his voyage was not established on voluntary consent?

• It is interesting to note the Scripture, "Where there is no vision, the people perish." Proverbs 29:18. How does the lack of vision in the sailors cause them to be discontent? How did Columbus endeavor to share the vision which he had with the sailors?

• *Student Activity Pages 12-7* and *12-8,* Begin a time line of Columbus's voyage. Students record the date of departure from Spain, "August 3, 1492." Cut and glue the picture of the three caravels. The time line will be completed in future lessons.

Columbus's Voyage

August 3, 1492	Columbus set sail from Spain
September 6, 1492	Nina, Pinta and Santa Maria sailed from the Canary Islands.
	Day after day, they saw no land.
October 11, 1492	Columbus saw a light. Land is sighted.
	Columbus claimed the land for Spain.
October 12, 1492	Columbus thanked God.

Leading Idea

Columbus recorded the Providential acts of God in his journal.

Student Text, page 65

• "When Columbus set sail on this memorable voyage, he commenced a regular journal, intended for the inspection of the Spanish sovereigns. . . .

"'In nomine D. N. Jesu Christi. Whereas most Christian, most high, most excellent and most powerful princes, king and queen of the Spains, and of the islands of the sea, our sovereigns, in the present year of 1492, after your highnesses had put an end to the war with the Moors who ruled in Europe . . . I departed . . . from the city of Granada, on Saturday, the 12th of May, of the same year 1492, to Palos, a seaport, where I armed three ships, well calculated for such service, and sailed from that port well furnished with provisions and with many seamen, on Friday, the third of August, of the same year, half an hour before sunrise, and took the route for the Canary Islands of your highnesses to steer my course thence, and navigate until I should arrive at the Indies . . . For this purpose I intend to write during this voyage, very punctually from day to day, all that I may do, and see, and experience, as will hereafter be seen. Also, my sovereign princes, besides describing each night all that has occurred in the day, and in the day the navigation of the night, I propose to make a chart in which I will set down the waters and lands of the Ocean sea in their proper situations under their bearings; and further, to compose a book, and illustrate the whole in picture . . . and upon the whole it will be essential that I should forget sleep and attend closely to the navigation to accomplish these things, which will be a great labor.' . . ."

Washington Irving, *The Life and Voyages of Christopher Columbus*

For Reflection and Reasoning

• Continue the time line, *Student Activity Pages 12-7* and *12-8*. Record, next to September 6, 1492, "Nina, Pinta, and Santa Maria sailed from the Canary Islands."

• Columbus recognized the importance of

recording the events and observations of the voyage. He was diligent in recording each day in his journal, see Columbus's opening to the journal. Note that he indicates he will "forget sleep" to "accomplish these things."

• Columbus wrote down each detail from the voyage. He included the weather, a description of the fish that swam near the ship and the birds that flew overhead.

• See *Student Activity Page 12-9.* The students could prepare a daily journal according to the style which Columbus

used. Columbus included observations of the weather, the winds, the fish and birds they saw, and the various plants that floated in the water.

Specify a certain number of days or weeks in which this journal will be kept. It may be best to make suggestions of the observations to be included. The exercise will sharpen the observation and writing skills, and will emphasize the importance of written records in preserving one's heritage, both individually and nationally. The students might decorate the pages with illustrations of selected observations.

Leading Idea

God Providentially encouraged Columbus through signs that land was ahead.

Student Text, pages 65-66

• "Early in the morning of the 6th of September Columbus set sail from the island of Gomera, and now might be said first to strike into the region of discovery; taking leave of these frontier islands of the Old World, and steering westward for the unknown parts of the Atlantic. For three days, however, a profound calm kept the vessels loitering with flagging sails within a short distance of the land.

"On losing sight of this last trace of land, the hearts of the crews failed them. They seemed literally to have taken leave of the world. Behind them was everything dear to the heart of man; country, family, friends, life itself; before them everything was chaos, mystery, and peril. In the perturbation of the moment, they despaired of ever more seeing their homes. Many of the rugged seamen shed tears, and some broke into loud lamentations. The admiral tried in every way to soothe their distress, and to inspire them with his own glorious anticipations. . . . He promised them land and riches, and everything that could arouse their cupid-

ity or inflame their imaginations, nor were these promises made for purposes of mere deception; he certainly believed that he should realize them all. . . .

"On the 14th of September the voyagers were rejoiced by the sight of what they considered harbingers of land. A heron, and a tropical bird . . . neither of which is supposed to venture far to sea, hovered about the ships. . . .

"They now began to see large patches of herbs and weeds drifting from the west, and increasing in quantity as they advanced. . . . They saw also a white tropical bird, of a kind which never sleeps upon the sea. . . .

"The crews were all in high spirits; each ship strove to get in the advance, and every seaman was eagerly on the look-out; for the sovereigns had promised a pension of ten thousand maravedis to him who should first discover land. . . .

"Notwithstanding his precaution to keep the people ignorant of the distance they had sailed, they were now growing extremely uneasy at the length of the voyage. They had advanced much farther west than ever man had sailed before, and though already beyond the reach of succor, still they continued daily leaving vast tracts of ocean behind them, and pressing onward and onward into that apparently boundless abyss. It is true they had been flattered by various indications of land, and still others were occurring; but all mocked them with vain hopes: after being hailed with a transient joy, they passed away, one after another, and the same interminable expanse of sea and sky continued to extend before them. Even the bland and gentle breeze, uniformly aft, was now conjured by their ingenious fears into a cause of alarm; for they began to imagine that the wind, in these seas, might always prevail from the east, and if so, would never permit their return to Spain.

"Columbus endeavored to dispel these gloomy presages sometimes by argument and expostulation, sometimes by awakening fresh hopes, and pointing out new signs of land. On the 20th of September the wind veered, with light breezes from the south-west. These, though adverse to their progress, had a cheering effect upon the people, as they proved that the wind did not always prevail from the east. . . .

"The minds of the crews, however, had gradually become diseased. They were full of vague terrors and superstitious fancies: they construed everything into a cause of alarm, and harassed their commander by incessant murmurs. . . .

"Columbus continued with admirable patience to reason with these fancies; . . .

"The situation of Columbus was daily becoming more and more critical. In proportion as he approached the regions where he expected to find land, the impatience of his crews augmented. The favorable signs which increased his confidence, were derided by them as delusive; and there was danger of their rebelling, and obliging him to turn back, when on the point of realizing the object of all his labors. . . .

"On the 25th of September the wind again became favorable, and they were able to resume their course directly to the west. . . . Martin Alonzo Pinzon mounted on the stern of his vessel crying 'Land! land! Senor I claim my reward!' He pointed at the same time to the southwest, where there was indeed an appearance of land at about twenty-five leagues' distance. Upon this Columbus threw himself on his knees and returned thanks to God; and Martin Alonzo repeated the *Gloria in excelsis,* in which he was joined by his own crew and that of the admiral.

". . . The morning light, however, put an end to all their hopes, as to a dream. The fancied land proved to be nothing but an evening cloud, and had vanished in the night. With dejected hearts they once more resumed their western course . . .

"On the 1st of October, according to the reckoning of the pilot of the admiral's ship, they had come five hundred and eighty leagues west of the Canary Islands. . . . On the following day the weeds floated from east to west; and on the third day no birds were to be seen.

"The crews now began to fear that they had passed between islands, from one to the other of which the birds had been flying. Columbus had also some doubts of the kind, but refused to alter his westward course. The people again uttered murmurs and menaces; but on the following day they were visited by such flights of birds, and the various indications of land became so numerous, that from a state of despondency they passed to one of confident expectation.

"Eager to obtain the promised pension, the seamen were continually giving the cry of land, on the least appearance of the kind. To put a stop to these false alarms, which produced continual disappointments, Columbus declared that should any one give such notice, and land not be discovered within three days afterward, he should thenceforth forfeit all claim to the reward.

"On the evening of the 6th of October, Martin Alonzo Pinzon began to lose confidence in their present course, and proposed that they should stand more to the southward. Columbus, however, still persisted in steering directly west. . . ."

Washington Irving, *The Life and Voyages of Christopher Columbus*

For Reflection and Reasoning

• What signs did Columbus and the men see which encouraged them they were near land? Why was it a discouragement?

• Why was the wind blowing from the east to the west helpful to them? Why did it cause fear?

• Columbus recorded in his Journal that he actually kept two reckonings. He made the one public, telling the men where he thought they were in their voyage. He kept the other to himself, as he thought the second reckoning would frighten the men. In reality the public reckoning was a more accurate calculation of the number of miles traveled.

• Why did each man want to be the first to see the land? How did this become a problem? What was Columbus's solution to the problem?

• Prepare an outdoor activity for the students. Place objects on the ground or up in the trees to represent the signs which encouraged the sailors that land was near—carved stick, leaves, flowers, birds, and a glimmering light. Each day,

have the students go outside and search for clues. Have a treat for the students to enjoy once they have arrived on land.

• On September 25, why were the men and Columbus so happy when they thought they saw land? What was their response? How does this demonstrate their understanding that God was in control of their voyage?

• Note how day after day they would think they saw land, and then there would be no land. Can you imagine how they felt? Did they know what was ahead?

• Continue the time line, *Student Activity Pages 12-7* and *12-8*. Cut and glue the picture of the sailor watching for land.

• Continue outlining and labeling the map. Draw a line to indicate the ship's voyage from Spain to the Canary Islands and then west.

Cultivating Student Mastery

1. Why did the sailors want to turn back?

Leading Idea

After long weeks of sailing, land was sighted at last, and God allowed the crew to arrive safely.

Student Text, pages 67-68

• "On the morning of the 7th of October, at sunrise, several of the admiral's crew thought they beheld land in the west, but so indistinctly that no one ventured to proclaim it . . . As they advanced, however, their cloud-built hopes faded away, and before evening the fancied land had again melted into the air.

"The crews now sank into a degree of dejection proportioned to their recent ex-

citement; but new circumstances occurred to arouse them. Columbus, having observed great flights of small field-birds going toward the south-west, concluded they must be secure of some neighboring land, where they would find food and a resting-place. . . . He had now come seven hundred and fifty leagues, the distance at which he had computed to find the island of Cipango; as there was no appearance of it, he might have missed it through some mistake in the latitude. He determined, therefore, on the evening of the 7th of October, to alter his course to the west-south-west, the direction in which the birds generally flew, and continue that direction for at least two days. . . .

"For three days they stood in this direction, and the further they went the more frequent and encouraging were the signs of land. . . .

"All these, however, were regarded by the crews as so many delusions beguiling them on to destruction; and when on the evening of the third day they beheld the sun go down upon a shoreless ocean, they broke forth into turbulent clamor. They exclaimed against this obstinacy in tempting fate by continuing on into a boundless sea. They insisted upon turning homeward, and abandoning the voyage as hopeless. . . .

"Columbus was now at open defiance with his crew, and his situation became desperate. Fortunately the manifestations of the vicinity to land were such on the following day as no longer to admit a doubt. Besides a quantity of fresh weeds, such as grow in rivers, they saw a green fish of a kind which keeps about rocks; then a branch of thorn with berries on it, and recently separated from the tree, floated by them; then they picked up a reed, a small board, and, above all, a staff artificially carved. All gloom and mutiny now gave way to sanguine expectation; and throughout the day each one was eagerly on the watch, in hopes of being the first to discover the long-sought-for land. . . .

"As the evening darkened, Columbus took his station on the top of the castle or cabin on the high poop of his vessel, ranging his eye along the dusky horizon, and maintaining an intense and unremitting watch. About ten o'clock he thought he beheld a light glimmering at a great distance. Fearing his eager hopes might deceive him, he called to Pedro Gutierrez, gentleman of the king's bedchamber, and inquired whether he saw such a light; the latter replied in the affirmative. Doubtful whether it might not yet be some delusion of the fancy, Columbus called Rodrigo Sanchez of Segovia, and made the same inquiry. By the time the latter had ascended the round-house the light had disappeared. They saw it once or twice afterward in sudden and passing gleams; as if it were a torch in the bark of a fisherman, rising and sinking with the waves; or in the hand of some person on shore, borne up and down as he walked from house to house. . . .

"They continued their course until two in the morning, when a gun from the Pinta gave the joyful signal of land. It was first descried by a mariner named Rodrigo de Triana; but the reward was afterward adjudged to the admiral, for having previously perceived the light. The land was now clearly seen about two leagues distant, whereupon they took in sail and lay to, waiting impatiently for the dawn."

Washington Irving, *The Life and Voyages of Christopher Columbus*

For Reflection and Reasoning

• Christopher Columbus possessed tremendous internal confidence in his plans to discover land. Because of this he was not swayed by external circumstances—either positive or negative. How did he endeavor to convey this to the crew? Why were they unable to possess the same internal confidence?

• At last, October 11, Columbus saw a light moving. He thought they must be near land. Do you think it was special for Columbus to be the first one to see the land? At 2:00 in the morning, the Pinta confirmed there was land. How long had they been sailing?

• Continue the time line, *Student Activity Pages 12-7* and *12-8*. Record: "Columbus saw a light. Land is sighted."

• Continue the map work. Complete the line for the voyage. Label San Salvador.

> **Leading Idea**
>
> ***All were happy to have arrived on the beautiful shore, where Columbus thanked the Lord for their safe voyage and claimed the land for Spain.***
>
> Student Text, pages 68-69

• "The thoughts and feelings of Columbus in this little space of time must have been tumultuous and intense. At length, in spite of every difficulty and danger, he had accomplished his object. The great mystery of the ocean was revealed; his theory, which had been the scoff of sages, was triumphantly established; he had secured to himself a glory durable as the world itself.

"It is difficult to conceive the feelings of such a man, at such a moment; or the conjectures which must have thronged upon his mind, as to the land before him, covered with darkness. . . .

"It was on Friday morning, the 12th of October, that Columbus first beheld the New World. As the day dawned he saw before him a level island, several leagues in extent, and covered with trees like a continual orchard. Though apparently un-cultivated, it was populous, for the inhabitants were seen issuing from all parts of the woods and running to the shore. They were perfectly naked, and, as they stood gazing at the ships, appeared by their attitudes and gestures to be lost in astonishment. Columbus made signal for the ships to cast anchor, and the boats to be manned and armed. He entered his own boat, richly attired in scarlet, and holding the royal standard; . . .

"On landing he threw himself on his knees, kissed the earth, and returned thanks to God with tears of joy. His example was followed by the rest, whose hearts indeed overflowed with the same feelings of gratitude. Columbus then rising drew his sword, displayed the royal standard, and assembling round him the two captains . . . he took solemn possession in the name of the Castilian sovereigns, giving the island the name of San Salvador. . . .

"The feelings of the crew now burst forth in the most extravagant transports. They had recently considered themselves devoted men, hurrying forward to destruction; they now looked upon themselves as favorites of fortune, and gave themselves up to the most unbounded joy. They thronged around the admiral with overflowing zeal, some embracing him, others kissing his hands. Those who had been most mutinous and turbulent during the voyage, were now most devoted and enthusiastic. Some begged favors of him, as if he had already wealth and honors in his gift. Many abject spirits who had outraged him by their insolence, now crouched at his feet, begging pardon for all the trouble they had caused him, and promising the blindest obedience for the future. . . .

"As Columbus supposed himself to have landed on an island at the extremity of India, he called the natives by the general appellation of Indians, . . .

"The islanders were friendly and gentle. Their only arms were lances, hardened at the end by fire, or pointed with a flint, or the teeth or bone of a fish. There was not iron to be seen, nor did they appear acquainted with its properties; for, when a drawn sword was presented to them, they unguardedly took it by the edge. . . .

"The avarice of the discoverers was quickly excited by the sight of small ornaments of gold, worn by some of the natives in their noses. These the latter gladly exchanged for glass beads and hawks' bells; and both parties exulted in the bargain, no doubt admiring each other's simplicity. . . .

"He inquired of the natives where this gold was procured. They answered him by signs, pointing to the south, where, he understood them, dwelt a king of such wealth that he was served in vessels of wrought gold. . . . He was persuaded that he had arrived among the islands described by Marco Polo as lying opposite to Cathay, in the Chinese sea, and he construed everything to accord with the account given of those opulent regions. . . . The country to the south, abounding in gold, could be no other than the famous island of Cipango; and the king who was served out of vessels of gold must be the monarch whose magnificent city and gorgeous palace, covered with plates of gold, had been extolled in such splendid terms by Marco Polo. . . "

Washington Irving, *The Life and Voyages of Christopher Columbus*

For Reflection and Reasoning

• What is the first view Columbus and his men have of the New World?

• What was Columbus's first act upon arrival in the New World? What was his second act? What does this tell us about why Columbus made the journey?

• Columbus began to give names to his discoveries. What did he call the people on the island? Why did he call them Indians? Where did Columbus think he was? Look at a map or globe and locate San Salvador. Also locate Cathay and the China Sea. How far was Columbus from where he thought he was?

• What was the name he gave to the island? San Salvador means Holy Saviour.

• The arrival of Columbus and his ships must have been a great surprise to the natives. Some historians indicate that Columbus's ship was the first large ship seen by the natives.

• What seemed to be of most interest to Columbus and his men?

• How did Columbus and his men treat the natives? How did the natives treat Columbus?

• Continue the time line, *Student Activity Pages 12-7* and *12-8*. Record: "October 12, 1492" and "Columbus thanked God." Cut and paste the picture of Columbus landing in the New World.

Leading Idea

A search for gold and a new plan

Student Text, pages 69-70

• "On the 19th [of November] Columbus again put to sea, . . .

". . . Speaking in his letters to the sovereigns . . . in his artless but enthusiastic language, '. . . render this country, most serene princes, of such marvellous beauty, that it surpasses all others in charms and graces, as the day doth the night in lustre. For which reason I often say to my people, that, much as I endeavor to give a complete account of it to your majesties, my tongue cannot express the whole truth, nor my pen describe it; and I have been so overwhelmed at the sight of so much beauty, that I have not known how to relate it.' . . .

"At eleven o'clock at night, being Christmas eve . . . Columbus, who had hitherto kept watch, finding the sea calm and smooth, and the ship almost motionless, retired to rest, not having slept the preceding night. He was, in general, extremely wakeful on his coasting voyages, passing whole nights upon deck in all weathers; never trusting to the watchfulness of others, where there was any difficulty or danger to be provided against. . . .

"No sooner had he retired than the steersman gave the helm in charge to one of the ship-boys, and went to sleep. This was in direct violation of an invariable order of the admiral, that the helm should never be intrusted to the boys. The rest of the mariners who had the watch took like advantage of the absence of Columbus, and in a little while the whole crew was buried in sleep. In the mean time the treacherous currents which run swiftly along this coast carried the vessel quietly, but with force, upon a sand-bank. The heedless boy had not noticed the breakers, although they made a roaring noise that might have been heard a league. No sooner, however, did he hear

the rudder strike, and hear the tumult of the rushing sea, than he began to cry for aid. Columbus, whose careful thoughts never permitted him to sleep profoundly, was the first on deck. The master of the ship, whose duty it was to have been on watch, next made his appearance, followed by others of the crew, half awake. . . .

"It was too late to save the ship, the current having set her more upon the bank. The admiral, seeing that his boat had deserted him, that the ship had swung across the stream, and that the water was continually gaining upon her, ordered the mast to be cut away, in the hope of lightening her sufficiently to float her off. Every effort was in vain. . . ."

Washington Irving, *The Life and Voyages of Christopher Columbus*

For Reflection and Reasoning

• Columbus sailed from island to island searching for gold.

• The Student Text does not give the details of the shipwreck. Using Irving's record, you may wish to expand the study for the students.

• When the Santa Maria was shipwrecked, what new plan did Columbus have? He hoped that the colony would be permanent and more settlers would come.

• The Student Text does not deal with

Columbus's future voyages. In God's Providence, the colony begun by Columbus did not last.

• Why was the fort necessary? How could the fort provide maximum protection?

• The students may build a fort using wooden building blocks.

Cultivating Student Mastery

1. When the Santa Maria was shipwrecked, what new plan did Columbus have?

Leading Idea

Divine Providence granted the wisdom, protection, and encouragement needed for the unique challenges of the return voyage.

Student Text, pages 70-71

• "It was on the 4th of January that Columbus set sail from La Navidad on his

return to Spain. . . .

"The trade-winds which had been so

propitious to Columbus on his outward voyage, were equally adverse to him on his return. . . .

"On the 12th of February, as they were flattering themselves with soon coming in sight of land, the wind came on to blow violently, with a heavy sea; they still kept their course to the east, but with great labor and peril . . . As the morning dawned of the 14th, there was a transient pause, and they made a little sail; but the wind rose again from the south with redoubled vehemence, raging throughout the day, and increasing in fury in the night . . . For three days they lay to, with just sail enough to keep them above the waves but the tempest still augmenting, they were obliged again to scud before the wind. . . .

"In the midst of these gloomy apprehensions, an expedient suggested itself, by which, though he and his ship should perish, the glory of his achievement might survive to his name, and its advantages be secured to his sovereigns. He wrote on parchment a brief account of his voyage and discovery, and of his having taken possession of the newly-found lands . . . This he sealed and directed to the king and queen; . . . He then wrapped it in a waxed cloth, which he placed in the centre of a cake of wax, and inclosing the whole in a large barrel, threw it into the sea . . . Lest this memorial should never reach the land he inclosed a copy in a similar manner, and placed it upon the poop, so that, should the caravel be swallowed up by the waves, the barrel might float off and survive. . . .

"On the morning of the 15th, at daybreak, the cry of land was given . . . The transports of the crew, at once more gaining sight of the Old World, were almost equal to those experienced on first be-

holding the New. . . . A nearer approach proved it to be an island; . . .

"Such were the difficulties and perils which attended his return to Europe; had one tenth part of them beset his outward voyage, his timid and factious crew would have risen in arms against the enterprise, and he never would have discovered the New World. . . .

"An ungenerous reception, however, awaited the poor tempest-tossed mariners on their first return to the abode of civilized men, far different from the sympathy and hospitality they had experienced among the savages of the New World. Scarcely had they begun their prayers and thanksgivings, when the rabble of the village, horse and foot, headed by the governor, surrounded the hermitage and took them all prisoners. . . .

"The King of Portugal, jealous lest the expedition of Columbus might interfere with his own discoveries, had sent orders to his commanders of islands and distant ports to seize and detain him whenever he should be met with. . . . Such was the first reception of the admiral on his return to the Old World, . . .

"Columbus gave an account of his voyage, and of the countries he had discovered. The king listened with much seeming pleasure, but with secret grief and mortification; reflecting that this splendid enterprise had once been offered to himself, and had been rejected. . . .

". . . [The king] did justice to the great merit of Columbus, and honored him as a distinguished benefactor of mankind; and he felt it his duty, as a generous prince, to protect all strangers driven by adverse fortune to his ports. . . ."

Washington Irving, *The Life and Voyages of Christopher Columbus*

For Reflection and Reasoning

• In many ways, the return trip held more difficulties than the outgoing voy-

age. As appropriate for the students, the teacher, using Irving's account, may expand the details included in the Student Text. Why was it Providential that the most difficult sailing occurred on the way home, rather than on the way to the Indies?

• A written record of firsthand experiences is an invaluable source by which a nation's history may be maintained. How did Columbus's actions prove that he understood this? Why are these writings so valuable today?

• When did Columbus arrive in Portugal? How long had they been gone?

• How did the events of his arrival in Portugal reconfirm for Columbus that Providence had directed him to receive support from Spain rather than Portugal as he made his voyages of discovery?

Cultivating Student Mastery

1. How did Columbus make sure others would know about the voyage?

Leading Idea

The enterprise was accomplished: To God be the glory

Student Text, pages 71-72

• "The triumphant return of Columbus was a prodigious event in the history of the little port of Palos, where everybody was more or less interested in the fate of his expedition. The most important and wealthy sea-captains of the place had engaged in it, and scarcely a family but had some relative or friend among the navigators. The departure of the ships upon what appeared a chimerical and desperate cruise, had spread gloom and dismay over the place; and the storms which had raged throughout the winter had heightened the public despondency. . . .

"Great was the agitation of the inhabitants, therefore, when they beheld one of the ships standing up the river; but when they learned that she returned in triumph from the discovery of a world, the whole community broke forth in transports of joy. The bells were rung, the shops shut, all business was suspended: for a time there was nothing but hurry and tumult. When Columbus landed the multitude thronged to see and welcome him, and a grand procession was formed to the principal church, to return thanks to God for so signal a discovery made by the people of that place— forgetting, in their exultation, the thousand difficulties they had thrown in the

way of the enterprise. Wherever Columbus passed, he was hailed with shouts and acclamations. What a contrast to his departure a few months before, followed by murmurs and execrations; or, rather, what a contrast to his first arrival at Palos, a poor pedestrian, craving bread and water for his child at the gate of a convent! . . .

"About the middle of April Columbus arrived at Barcelona, where every preparation had been made to give him a solemn and magnificent reception. . . . It seemed as if the public eye could not be sated with gazing on these trophies of an unknown world; or on the remarkable man by whom it had been discovered. There was a sublimity in this event that mingled a solemn feeling with the public joy. It was looked upon as a vast and signal dispensation of Providence, in reward for the piety of the monarchs; and the majestic and venerable appearance of the discoverer, so different from the youth and buoyancy generally expected from roving enterprise, seemed in harmony with the grandeur and dignity of his achievement.

"To receive him with suitable pomp and distinction, the sovereigns had ordered their throne to be placed in public

98   *Copyright © Ruth Smith*

under a rich canopy of brocade of gold . . . Here the king and queen awaited his arrival, seated in state . . . At length Columbus entered the hall, surrounded by a brilliant crowd of cavaliers, among whom . . . he was conspicuous for his stately and commanding person, which with his countenance, rendered venerable by his gray hairs, gave him the august appearance of a senator of Rome; a modest smile lighted up his features, showing that he enjoyed the state and glory in which he came; and certainly nothing could be more deeply moving to a mind inflamed by noble ambition, and conscious of having greatly deserved, than these testimonials of the admiration and gratitude of a nation, or rather of a world. As Columbus approached the sovereigns rose, as if receiving a person of the highest rank. Bending his knees, he offered to kiss their hands; but there was some hesitation on their part to permit this act of homage. Raising him in the

most gracious manner, they ordered him to seat himself in their presence; a rare honor in this proud and punctilious court.

"At their request he now gave an account of the most striking events of his voyage, and a description of the islands discovered. . . .

"When he had finished, the sovereigns sank on their knees, and raising their clasped hands to heaven, their eyes filled with tears of joy and gratitude, poured forth thanks and praises to God for so great a providence; all present followed their example; a deep and solemn enthusiasm pervaded that splendid assembly, and prevented all common acclamations of triumph. . . . Such was the solemn and pious manner in which the brilliant court of Spain celebrated this sublime event; offering up a grateful tribute of melody and praise, and giving glory to God for the discovery of another world. . . ."

Washington Irving, *The Life and Voyages of Christopher Columbus*

For Reflection and Reasoning

• When Columbus returned to Spain, how did the people of Spain honor him?

• How was Columbus's Christian character evident when he was honored for his success?

• Consider the character of King Ferdinand and Queen Isabella. What were their reasons for helping Columbus?

• What was their response to Columbus's arrival at the court? What was their response to his discoveries?

• See *Student Activity Pages 12-10* and *12-11*. Reason from the Student Text to answer the questions of how Columbus, the sailors, and the King and Queen honored the Hand of God. Cut and glue the pictures of the men at the church and Columbus before the King and Queen.

Leading Idea

Christopher Columbus — Link to the New World

Student Text, page 72

• "The joy occasioned by the great discovery of Columbus was not confined to Spain; the tidings were spread far and wide by the communications of ambassa-

dors, the correspondence of the learned, the negotiations of merchants, and the reports of travellers, and the whole civilized world was filled with wonder and delight . . . The news was brought to Genoa and was recorded among the triumphant events of the year; for the republic, though she may have slighted the opportunity of making herself mistress of the discovery, has ever since been tenacious of the glory of having given birth to the discoverer. . . .

"Every member of civilized society, in fact, rejoiced in the occurrence, as one in which he was more or less interested. To some it opened a new and unbounded field of inquiry; to others, of enterprise; and every one awaited with intense eagerness the further development of this unknown world, still covered with mystery, the partial glimpses of which were so full of wonder. . . .

"During the whole of his sojourn at Barcelona, the sovereigns took every occasion to bestow on Columbus personal marks of their high consideration. He was admitted at all times to the royal presence, and the queen delighted to converse with him on the subject of his enterprises. . . . To perpetuate in his family the glory of his achievement, a coat of arms was assigned him, in which the royal arms, the castle and lion, were quartered with his proper bearings, which were a group of islands surrounded by waves. To these arms was afterward annexed the motto:

To Castile and Leon
Columbus gave a new world."

For Reflection and Reasoning

● Review: What is the Old World? What is the New World?

● Review: What is History?

● History shows how God uses men and nations to accomplish His plan. What individuals and nations were used by God to help Columbus reach the New World? What were the contributions of each?

● The students could write a short essay describing a particular aspect of the study of Columbus. Topics might include: Why was Columbus called a hero of Spain? How did Columbus earn the title, "Admiral of the Ocean Sea"?

● Although Columbus was searching for the Indies, God used him to find the way to the New World. Did Columbus ever know the true value of his discovery?

Supplemental Activities

● Visit a museum in which rope making or sailing are illustrated. If this is not possible, check with libraries, etc., for videos, pictures, or diagrams showing the skills and excitement of sailing.

● Prepare a re-enactment of Columbus's parade before the King and Queen of Spain. Write a simple script for Columbus, Queen Isabella, King Ferdinand, and possibly the King of Portugal. Use imagination in making it an enjoyable and memorable event. Students may wish to invite their parents to attend the festivity.

PILGRIM
Seed of our Christian Republic
Chapters 13-14
3-5 Weeks

Chapter 13
The Earliest Settlement in the New World
Jamestown
5-7 Days

> **Leading Idea**
>
> ***God preserved North America until He had a people ready.***
>
> Student Text, page 73

• Christopher Columbus opened the door to the New World. But it was not until the explorations of the English, under the direction of John Cabot, that the mainland of North America was discovered and claimed.

Why England? The Bible had been in the hands of the people in England since Wycliffe's translation of 1382. They had reasoned from the Scriptures concerning their personal relationship to God and identified principles of church government. God had prepared them to extend Biblical principles into the sphere of civil government.

For Reflection and Reasoning

• Review: Using a map or globe, recall the route of Christopher Columbus's voyages. What did Columbus think was his destination? Did he ever know that he had discovered a New World?

Who guided Columbus's ships through storms and over the vast ocean?

• Use a map to identify the voyage of Cabot and the discovery of the mainland of North America. When the English began to explore, John Cabot found the mainland of North America. Who guided Cabot's ship?

• Why did God preserve the mainland of North America for the English? If Spain had claimed North America, who would have controlled it? What church would have been established in North America? The people of England had the Bible in their hands since 1382.

• Use the chart below to compare/contrast England and Spain. This chart

Spain	England
•Controlled by a King and Queen	•Controlled by a King
•The Bible is only in the Church	•The people have the Bible in their own homes

may be recorded in the student's notebook.

Leading Idea

When a people have little self government, they will have much external government.

Student Text, pages 74-75

• Locate Jamestown and the James River on a map.

• Review: What is self government? What is civil government? What is the relationship between self government and the amount of external government. See Teacher's Guide, page 26.

• What did the King decide concerning the beginning of the colony? What did the people decide? Did the King expect the people to be able to govern themselves?

• Using *Student Activity Page 13-1*, make a list of the King's rules for the colony.

• Why were most of the men who arrived in Jamestown not prepared for what would be required of them? Why did they come? What was their plan?

The King's Rules for Jamestown

The King -

Made the civil government

Chose the rulers

Chose the church

Controlled the money

The people had to obey the King's rules.

Cultivating Student Mastery

1. How did the King show that he thought the men would not be self governed?

2. Why was it so hard for the men in Jamestown?

Leading Idea

God prepares individuals for His purpose — John Smith

Student Text, pages 75-76

• The orders for the colony's governing Council were sent on the ship in a sealed box. When the box was opened and the list was read, John Smith's name was included on the Council. At first, the other members refused to allow Smith to be a part of that Council. After facing great difficulties, the colonists recognized that John Smith had the qualities of leadership needed to give the colony direction.

"But however well chosen the situation might be, the members of the colony were far from availing themselves of its advantages. Violent animosities had broke out among some of their leaders, during their voyage to Virginia. These did not subside on their arrival there. The first deed of the council, which assumed the government in virtue of a commission brought from England under the seal of the company, and opened on the day after they landed, was an act of injustice. Captain Smith, who had been appointed a member of the council, was excluded from his seat at the board . . . This diminution of his influence, and restraint on his activity, was an essential injury to the colony, . . .

"To this was added a calamity still more dreadful; the stock of provisions left for their subsistence, on the departure of their ships for England (June 15), was so scanty and of such bad quality, that a scarcity, approaching almost to absolute famine, soon followed. Such poor unwholesome fare brought on diseases, the violence of which was so much increased by the sultry heat of the climate, and the moisture of a country covered with wood, that before the beginning of September one half of their number died, and most of the survivors were sickly and dejected. . . Every eye was now turned towards Smith, and all willingly devolved on him that authority of which they had formerly deprived him . . ."[19]

William Robertson, *History of the Discovery and Settlement of America*

These details were not included in the Student Text. The teacher may expand the material provided as felt appropriate.

• God gave John Smith the leadership qualities which would be required in Jamestown.

"It is not too much to say, that had not Captain Smith of Willoughby, strove, fought, and endured as he did, the present United States of America might never have come into existence.

"To what one single cause, under GOD, can be assigned the preservation of the James River Settlement after the early death of Captain Bartholomew Gosnold, on 22 August 1607, but to the fortunate presence of this English Captain, so self-denying, so energetic, so full of resources, and so trained (by his conflicts and captivity in Eastern Europe) in dealing with the savage races?"[20]

Edward Arber, *The Settlement of Jamestown*

For Reflection and Reasoning

• John Smith was prepared to give the men of Jamestown the leadership they needed. In what ways did he direct the colony as they were building?

• Consider the picture of the Jamestown colony on pages 74-75 of the Student Text. Discuss the tasks required to build the houses. What did they build for protection? Why did they build their settlement on the shore of the river?

• What is thatch? What does it mean to thatch a house? Why was thatch used? What is on your house rather than thatch?

• John Smith tried to make friends with the Indians. Why was it important for the people of Virginia to have the Indians as their friends?

• Reason with the students to compile a list of John Smith's activities as leader of the colony. Consider that God had prepared him for these tasks.
 • He helped them build homes
 • He explored the nearby country
 • He made friends with the Indians
This list could be included as Student Notes.

• What qualities of character can be identified in the life of John Smith?

Cultivating Student Mastery

1. What qualities made John Smith a good leader for Jamestown?

God prepares individuals for His purpose — Pocahontas

Student Text, pages 76-77

• Many early historians record John Smith's encounter with Powhatan. Note the following record:

"At last they brought him to *Meronocomoco,* where was *Powhatan* their Emperor. Here more than two hundred of those grim Courtiers stood wondering at him, as he had been a monster; till *Powhatan* and his train had put themselves in their greatest braveries. Before a fire upon a seat like a bedstead, he sat covered with a great robe. . .

"At his entrance before the king, all the people gave a great shout. The Queen of *Appamatuck* was appointed to bring him water to wash his hands, and another brought him a bunch of feathers, in stead of a Towel to dry them: hav-

ing feasted him after their best barbarous manner they could, a long consultation was held, but the conclusion was, two great stones were brought before *Powhatan:* then as many as could laid hands on him, dragged him to them, and thereon laid his head, and being ready with their clubs, to beat out his brains, *Pocahontas* the Kings dearest daughter, when no entreaty could prevail, got his head in her arms, and laid her own upon his to save him from death: whereat the Emperor was contented he should live to make him hatchets, and her bells, beads, and copper; for they thought him as well of all occupations as themselves. . ."[21]
Thomas Studley, Robert Fenton, Edward Harrington, and John Smith, *The Settlement of Jamestown*

• What is a compass? What might have John Smith shown the Indians that the compass could do?

• Demonstrate the use of a compass for the students. A modern compass is

somewhat different than the compass John Smith would have given the Indian King, but the concept would have been the same.

• When John Smith went to the various

Indian tribes, he was sometimes considered a friend, and sometimes an enemy. God had prepared the heart of Pocahontas to be a friend to John Smith. If she had not been his friend, what would have happened to John Smith?

● How did Pocahontas continue to be a friend to the people at Jamestown? During her many visits the people grew to love her.

● The students will enjoy considering the portraits of John Smith and Pocahontas.

Cultivating Student Mastery

1. How did God use Pocahontas to help the Jamestown colony? Students may draw a picture of Pocahontas helping the Jamestown colony.

Leading Idea

Lack of self government hampered the Jamestown colony.

Student Text, page 78

● "If Smith had died, or left, earlier than he did; the James river Settlement must have succumbed: for manifestly he was the life and energy of the whole Plantation. If the Third Supply, on their arrival there, in August 1609 had found an abandoned, or a destroyed Colony: that they alone could not have succeeded, where Smith would have failed, is quite evident from the fact that they *did* all but perish through *The Starving Time,* in spite of all the resources, which he left ready to their hands, at his going home, after he had been accidentally blown up by gunpowder, on the 4th of October 1609."[22]

Edward Arber,
The Settlement of Jamestown

For Reflection and Reasoning

● Under John Smith's leadership, Jamestown grew. The settlers still had not learned to govern themselves. How was their lack of self government shown when John Smith was wounded and had to return to England?

● Lack of self government characterized the Jamestown colonists. For discussion, develop a chart contrasting Jamestown under John Smith's strong leadership with the "rack and ruin" after Smith returned to England. Review the ideas regarding the amount of external government required when people are not self governed. *The chart is too lengthy for the students to record.*

Under John Smith	After John Smith Returned to England
The people were lazy and did not govern themselves.	There was no strong leader.
He controlled the men and made them work.	The people would not work hard.
Because John Smith was such a strong leader, the colony was orderly and grew.	Wasteful.
	After 6 months, only 60 people were left.
	The colonists wanted to leave Jamestown.

The people's hearts did not change. Without strong external government, the colony almost starved.

Leading Idea

The Jamestown Colony prepared the way for the Pilgrims to come to North America.

Student Text, pages 78-80

• Although the Jamestown colony was not a permanent settlement, the efforts of John Smith and the other settlers were a stepping stone for the colonization of America. John Smith's maps and his writings of the history of Virginia encouraged others to consider the opportunities of the New World.

For Reflection and Reasoning

• How did Pocahontas's friendship with the Jamestown colony affect her life?

• John Smith prepared maps of Virginia. Were these maps totally accurate? How did they benefit future settlers? Compare the copy of John Smith's map of Virginia with a modern map of Virginia. What wrong ideas did John Smith have about the geography of Virginia?

• John Smith, along with others, wrote a *General History of Virginia.* How did this benefit future settlers?

• Use *Student Activity Page 13-2* for a review, confirming the relationship of the Bible being made available to the people of England, with the settlement of North America.

God Had a Plan for the North American Continent

1382	Wycliffe Bible in English
Who was the link to the New World? 1492	Christopher Columbus
What explorer claimed North America for England? 1497	John Cabot
	England claimed North America. There were no English colonies in the new land.
1536	Tyndale Bible in England
Who wanted to settle the first colony in North America? 1578	Sir Walter Raleigh
What colony was planned and begun under the King's laws? 1607	Jamestown

Chapter 14
The Pilgrims
Seed of Our Christian Republic
10-15 Days

> **Leading Idea**
>
> ## God worked in the nation of England to prepare the way for the Pilgrims.
>
> Student Text, page 81

• The history of the Pilgrims must be considered in light of the history of the Bible in the hands of the people and its relationship to the church and the nation.

Before Wycliffe and Tyndale translated the Scriptures, the Bible was only found in the Roman churches. Even there it was only read and studied by a few.

It was under the authority of King Henry VIII that Tyndale was martyred. However, God used King Henry VIII to approve the publication of the Tyndale Bible for sale to the people of England.

To achieve his own purpose, King Henry VIII separated England from the Roman Church and made himself the head of a new church — the Church of England. The teachings of the Church of England differed little from the Church of Rome.

Proverbs 21:1 teaches that the heart of the King is in God's hand. This can be seen in the life of Henry VIII.

"In sum, God's ways are a great deep; who has often showed his power and wisdom in raising up unlikely and unpromising instruments to do great services in the world; not always employing the best men in them, lest good instruments should share too deep in the praises of that, which is only due to the supreme Creator and Governor of the world: and therefore he will stain the pride of all glory, that such as glory may only glory in the Lord."[23]

Gilbert Burnet, D.D., *The History of the Reformation of the Church of England*

• To prepare the students, review the events which produced the Pilgrims. How were the churches of the New Testament governed? See Student Text, Chapter 11. Under what church did the churches of Europe choose to be governed? Review *Student Activity Page 11-3.* By the time of Tyndale, the Roman

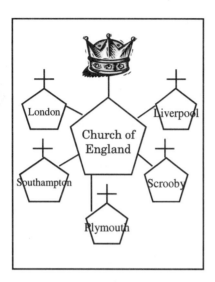

Church governed the churches even in England.

King Henry VIII did not want to be a part of the Church of Rome. He set up a new church in England. It was called the Church of England.

Use *Student Activity Page 14-1*, to identify the structure in the Church of England. Draw a cross on each church. Draw a line from the crown, representing the King of England, to the Church of England. Then draw lines from each church to the Church of England.

• Using the two *Student Activity Pages 14-1* and *11-3*, compare the Church of Rome, with the Church of England. How are they alike? How are they different?

Leading Idea

The Bible in the hands of the people changed history.

Student Text, pages 82-83

• William Bradford in his *History of Plimouth Plantation* records the change which occurred in the hearts of the people when they had the Bible in their hands: "But that I may come more near my indentmente; when as by the travell & diligence of some godly & zealous preachers, & Gods blessing on their labours, as in other places of ye land, so in ye North parts, many became inlightened by ye word of God, and had their ignorance & sins discovered unto them, and begane by his grace to reforme their lives, the worke of God was no sooner manifest in them, but presently they were both scoffed and scorned by ye prophane multitude, and ye ministers urged with ye yoak of subscription, or els must be silenced; and ye poore people were so vexed with apparators, & pursuants, & ye comissarie courts, as truly their affliction was not smale; which, notwithstanding, they bore sundrie years with much patience, till they were occasioned (by ye continuance & encrease of these troubles, and other means which ye Lord raised up in those days) to see further into things by the light of ye word of God. . . So many therfore of these proffessors as saw ye evill of these things, in thes parts, and whose harts ye Lord had touched with heavenly Zeale for his trueth, they shooke of this yoake of antichristian bondange, and as ye Lords free people, joyned them selves (by a covenant of the Lord) into a church estate, in ye felowship of ye gospell, to walke in all his wayes, make known or to be made known unto them, according to their best endeavours, whatsoever it should cost them, the Lord assisting them."[24]

• Noah Webster defines a separatist as "One that withdraws from a church, or rather from an established church, to which he has belonged."

For Reflection and Reasoning

• How did the Bible in English cause the people of England to change? What did they learn first from the Bible? Once their hearts were changed, how did it change their lives?

• As the people studied the Bible, they read about the New Testament churches. How were these churches different from the churches in England? Who controlled what was taught in the Church of England? Why did the Separatists believe they could have their own church?

• Use *Student Activity Page 14-2*, to identify the changes which occurred as the Bible was in the hands of the individual in England.

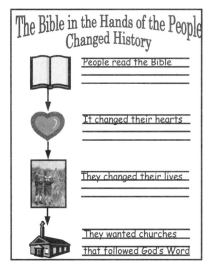

The Bible in the Hands of the People Changed History

People read the Bible

It changed their hearts

They changed their lives

They wanted churches that followed God's Word

Cultivating Student Mastery

1. How did reading the Bible change some of the people in England?

2. Why did the Separatists believe they could have their own church?

Leading Idea

God's Providence in the Separatists move to Holland

Student Text, pages 83-84

• The Scrooby congregation chose Holland as their new home, because they knew they could worship God according to their own conscience.

• William Bradford recorded the Separatists concerns with moving to Holland and the difficulties they would face there. "But these things did not dismay them (though they did some times trouble them) for their desires were sett on ye ways of God, & to injoye his ordinances; but they rested on his providence, & knew whom they had beleeved."[25] Their trust was in the Lord and His Providential care.

• The small congregation made several attempts to leave England but encountered many difficulties. The teacher may expand upon these details as appropriate for the students. ". . . I might relate many other notable passages and troubles which they endured and underwente. . . Yet I may not omitte ye fruit that came hearby, for by these so publick troubles, in so many eminente places, their became famouss. . . And their godly cariage & Christian behaviour was such as left a deep impression in the minds of many."[26]

For Reflection and Reasoning

• Review: What is a Separatist? Why were these people called Separatists? Why did they want to separate from the Church of England?

• Reason from the Student Text to help

Difficulties the Separatists would face in Holland

They did not speak Dutch

They could not be farmers

the students make a list of the difficulties which the Separatists knew they would face in Holland. *Student Activity Page 14-3.*

• The Separatists knew that life in Holland would be very difficult.

• The King made it difficult for them to leave England, even though he said he wanted them to leave. Why were they willing to endure all of these difficulties in order to go to Holland? What gave them the courage to do it?

• Look at a map of Europe to find Scrooby, England and Holland. Note the length of the voyage from England to Holland by sea.

Leading Idea

Character is produced through difficulties

Student Text, pages 84-85

• Webster defines character as "The peculiar qualities, impressed by nature or habit on a person, which distinguish him from others . . ."

• Each individual's character is formed through difficulties and challenges.

In another definition, Webster states that character is "A mark made by cutting or engraving, as on stone, metal or other hard material. . ." This *mark* literally refers to the mark made by printing. But it can also be applied to the mark made upon the individual as he internalizes Biblical principles and ideals and deals with difficulties in his life.

The Separatists endured imprisonment, betrayal, confiscation of property,

and separation from their wives and children, to protect their liberty of conscience. They left their beloved England for Holland to seek the liberty to worship God according to His Word.

The hardness of life in Holland further prepared this small band of Separatists for America and the difficulties to be faced in that new land.

• William Bradford identified the reasons for the departure from Holland. He identified 1) The hardness of life, which discouraged others from joining them; 2) Premature physical aging; 3) Children suffered greatly and some were drawn away to the Dutch life. 4) But, that which seems more important is the last reason given: "Lastly, (and which was

not least,) a great hope & inward zeall they had of laying some good foundation, or at least to make some way therunto, for ye propagating & advancing ye gospell of ye kingdom of Christ in those remote parts of ye world; yea, though they should be but even as stepping-stones unto others for ye performing of so great a work."[27]

*** ***

For Reflection and Reasoning

• Why was life in Holland difficult for the Separatists? What character was evident in their lives? Why did the Dutch want to hire them?

• Why did the Separatists consider moving to America?

• How long would the trip to America take? Would they be able to go back to Holland or England very easily?

• Although the Student Text does not identify the location of the Separatists in Holland, point out Amsterdam and Leyden on a map of Holland. The congregation arrived in Amsterdam and lived there for about one year. They then moved to Leyden. Why would life in Leyden be even more difficult than life in Amsterdam?

• Looking at a globe, compare the distance from England to Holland with the distance from Holland to America.

• Using the Student Text, list the Pilgrims reasons for leaving Holland and going to America. *Student Activity Page 14-4.* The map will be labeled during a later lesson.

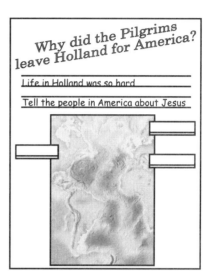

Cultivating Student Mastery

1. Why were the Separatists willing to face these difficulties?

Leading Idea

The Separatist becomes a Pilgrim.

Student Text, page 85

• Webster defines a pilgrim as "A wanderer; a traveler; particularly, one that travels to a distance from his own country to visit a holy place. . ." Why were the Separatists called Pilgrims? Why were the Jamestown settlers not called Pilgrims?

Might we conclude that the desire of the Separatist congregation to *advance the kingdom of Christ in those remote parts of the world* earned them the distinction of the title *Pilgrims?* They saw themselves as *stepping stones* for others who would follow after them.

For Reflection and Reasoning

• Would life be difficult in America? How did they know? What difficulties might they encounter in America? Consider the problems that the Jamestown settlers had faced.

• Pastor Robinson planned to join them later in America. Why would it have been very difficult for the Pilgrims to settle in America without their Pastor?

• What is a Pilgrim? Why were these Separatists called Pilgrims?

• Label England, Holland, and America on the map, *Student Activity Page 14-4.*

Cultivating Student Mastery

1. What is a Pilgrim?

2. Why were these Separatists called Pilgrims?

Leading Idea

Preparations for America

Student Text, pages 85-86

• Preparations for the voyage and settlement in the New World demanded much from this small band of Pilgrims. A patent was received from the King for a settlement in Virginia, and the ships were hired.

The venture company that financed the voyage, required that all properties were to be held in common for seven years. The company was to be repaid from this common storehouse.

"3. The persons transported & ye adventurers shall continue their joynt stock & partnership together, ye space of 7. Years, (excepte some unexpected im-

pedimente doe cause ye whole company to agree otherwise,) during which time, all profits & benefits that are gott by trade, traffick, trucking, working, fishing, or any other means of any person or persons, remaine still in ye comone stock until ye division."[28]

The company also enlisted volunteers to join the small band of Separatists. These additional settlers were not of the same church background and many were not Christians. Many historians describe the settlers as *saints* and *strangers*.

For Reflection and Reasoning

• Note: 1) A number of settlers were enlisted to join the Separatists. These families were not necessarily Christians. 2) All of the property was to be held in common. This added to the difficulties

later in the new settlement.

• As the plans for the trip to America were completed, two ships were hired — the Speedwell and Mayflower. Why was it best for more than one ship to make the long voyage acoss the ocean?

God's protection during the voyage to America

Student Text, pages 86-87

• None could have imagined the difficulties that would occur during the ocean voyage. The two ships set out, but soon had to return to England, because the Speedwell had sprung a leak. The Speedwell was considered unfit for the voyage. Bradford related that some chose not to complete the voyage either out of discontent or fear. He then stated, "And thus, like Gedions armie, this small number was devided, as if ye Lord by this worke of his providence thought these few to many for ye great worke he had to doe." Regarding the difficulty with the Speedwell, Bradford observed: "But here by the way let me show, how afterward it was found yt the leaknes of this ship was partly by being over masted, and too much pressed with sayles; for after she made many viages & performed her service very sufficinetly, to ye great profite of he owners. But more espetially, by the cuning & deceite of ye mr. & his company, who were hired to stay a whole year in ye cuntrie, and now fancying dislike & fearing wante of victeles, they ploted this strategem to free them selves; as afterwards was knowne, & by some of them confessed. . ."[29]

• The Mayflower voyage was extremely difficult. The Pilgrims endured the severe storms and the constraint of being kept below deck.

For Reflection and Reasoning

• The long trip across the ocean was very difficult. What made it so hard? Were additional people crowded onto the ship? Why? How long was the trip? What sometimes happens when people travel on a ship? Do they get sick? Might these people have gotten seasick? When there were storms, what did the Captain require of them?

• Review: Who controls the wind and weather? Read verses that confirm God's control of the weather. For example, Matthew 8:23-27, where Christ rebuked the wind and the sea.

• The Mayflower was a very small ship. Over 100 people were crowded on the lower deck. If a large open area is available, mark off the size of the Mayflower (approximately 90' x 125') and have the students try to imagine 100 men, women, boys, girls, and babies living there for over two months. They had very little space for sleeping, eating, and playing.

• The students may not understand the length of time from September 6, when the Pilgrims finally left England, to November 11, when they arrived at Cape Cod. Look at a calendar and discuss the events that have happened in the classroom or at home during the past two months. Have the students imagine what it would have been like to live on board the small ship for that length of time.

• Color a picture of the Mayflower. *Student Activity Page 14-5.*

Leading Idea

God's Providence in landing at Cape Cod

Student Text, pages 87-88

• Upon arrival in America, the Pilgrims found that they had been blown far from their original destination of Virginia. They recognized they were at Cape Cod. Efforts were made to sail to Virginia, but it was determined that they must find a place to settle near where they had landed.

It is difficult to imagine the arrival of these families in this new land, with none to welcome them and no place to go. "Being thus passed ye vast ocean, and a sea of troubles before in their preparation . . .they had now no friends to wellcome them, nor inns to entertaine or refresh their weatherbeaten bodies, no houses or much less townes to repaire too, to seeke for succoure. It is recorded in scripture as a mercie to ye apostle & his shipwraked company, yt the barbarians shewed them no smale kindnes in refreshing them, but these savage barbarians, when they mette with them (as after will appeare) were readier to fill their sids full of arrows then otherwise. And for ye season it was winter, and they that know ye winters of yt cuntrie know them to be sharp & violent, & subjecte to cruell & feirce stormes, deangerous to travill to known places, much more to serch an unknown coast. Besids, what could they see but a hidious & desolate wildernes, full of wild beasts & wild men? And what multituds ther might be of them they knew not. Neither could they, as it were, goe up to ye tope of Pisgah, to vew from this willdernes a more goodly cuntrie to feed their hops; for which way soever they turnd their eyes (save upward to ye heavens) they could have litle solace or content in respecte of any outward objects. . . What could now sustaine them but ye spirite of God & his grace? May not & ought not the children of these fathers rightly say: Our faithers were Englishmen which came over this great ocean, and were ready to perish in this willdernes; but they cried unto ye Lord, and he heard their voyce, and looked on their adversitie, &c."[30]

• A few explored the area with a small shallop. They found an area that had been cleared by an Indian tribe, but abandoned.

Their faith was in God's leading and certainly He had prepared a place for them.

For Reflection and Reasoning

• Locate Cape Cod on a map. Some say Cape Cod is like a finger beckoning people to its shore. Note on the map how far they were from the settlement in Virginia. Reason concerning the distance, the time of year, and why it was necessary for them to build their houses where they were.

• When the Mayflower arrived in America, the Pilgrims realized they were at Cape Cod, not Virginia. Who had guided their ship across the ocean? Where did He intend for them to settle?

• What would the weather have been

like at Cape Cod in November? If they had arrived in Virginia, would there have already been some other settlers? How was settling at Cape Cod more difficult than settling in Virginia? How did their finding a deserted Indian village show God's Providence?

1. What is Providence?

2. How did God provide for the Pilgrims in a special way when they arrived in Cape Cod?

Leading Idea

The Pilgrims established the first self governing colony.

Student Text, page 89

• As the small band of Pilgrims prepared to settle in the new land, they faced a dilemma. Their patent from the King had been granted for Virginia, but they had arrived in Cape Cod. The government and rules established under the patent did not apply. "I shall a little returne backe and begine with a combination made by them before they came ashore, being ye first foundation of their govermente in this place; occasioned partly by ye discontented & mutinous speeches that some of the strangers amongst them had let fall from them in ye ship—That when they came a shore they would use their owne libertie; for none had power to comand them, the patente they had being for Virginia, and not for New-england, which belonged to an other Government, with which ye Virginia Company had nothing to doe. And partly that shuch an acte by them done (this their condition considered) might be as firme as any patent, and in

some respects more sure."[31]

• God, in His wisdom, brought the small ship to a place without an established form of civil government. With the Separatists understanding of Biblical principles of self government and church government, they were prepared to extend those principles into the establishment of civil government.

• The Pilgrims desired to be *stepping stones* for others. The voluntary choice of a form of civil government was the first, major stepping stone for establishing the first nation built upon the idea of self-government.

The small seed of local self government planted in Plymouth grew during the next 150 years to become the basis of a new nation

• The Mayflower Compact will be studied at a later year.

For Reflection and Reasoning

• Review the idea that individual Christian self government will be extended into the external spheres: the

family, church, and civil government. See Teacher's Guide, page 54. Note the steps in the lives of the Pilgrims.
1. Bible in the hands of the individual
2. Individual salvation and Christian

self government
3. Independent self governing church
4. Self government in the colony

• What is self government? How can a colony be a self governing colony?

1. How did the Pilgrims show that they did not need a King to govern them?

Leading Idea

"*America's heritage of Christian character*" — *brotherly love and Christian care*

Student Text, pages 89-90

• Bradford described the difficulties of the first winter in Plymouth: "But that which was most sadd & lamentable was, that in 2. or 3. moneths time halfe of their company dyed, espetialy in Jan. & February, being ye depth of winter, and wanting houses & other comforts; being infected with ye scurvie & other diseases, which this long vioage & their inacomodate condition had brought upon them; so as ther dyed some times 2. or 3. of a day, in ye foresaid time; that of 100. & odd persons, scarce 50. remained. And of these in ye time of most distres, ther was but 6. or 7. sound persons, who, to their great comendations be it spoken, spared no pains, night nor day, but with abundance of toyle and hazard of their owne health, fetched them woode, made them fires, drest them meat, made their beads, washed their lothsome cloaths, cloathed, & uncloathed them; in a word, did all ye homly & necessarie offices for them wch dainty & quesie stomacks cannot endure to hear named; and all this willingly & cherfully, without any grudging in ye least, shewing herein their true love unto their friends & bretheren. A rare example & worthy to be remembered. Two of these 7. were Mr. William Brewster, ther reverend Elder, & Myles Standish, ther Captein & military comander, unto whom my selfe, & many others, were much beholden in our low & sicke condition. And yet the Lord so upheld these persons, as in this generall calamity they were not at all infected either with sicknes, or lamnes. And what I have said of these, I may say of many others who dyed in this generall vissitation, & others yet living, that whilst they had health, yea, or any strength, continuing, they were not wanting to any that had need of them. And I doute not but their recompence is with ye Lord . . ."[32]

• America's form of government — a republic — demands a certain character in the people. Rosalie Slater, in the volume *Teaching and Learning America's Christian History,* identified the principle, "America's Heritage of Christian Character,"[33] and its evidence in the lives of the Pilgrims. Brotherly love and Christian care have been selected for emphasis during this year of study.

• Webster defines love as "An affection of the mind" and Brotherly love as "affectionate, kind." And care as "concern; anxiety; solicitude . . . with a view to safety or protection." Christian care would be *of or pertaining to Christ.* The two great commandments of the New Testament teach that we must love our neighbor as ourself. Certainly this provides the highest standard of Brotherly love and Christian care.

For Reflection and Reasoning

• Reason with the students concerning the relationship of *Brotherly love* and *Christian care*. Label *Student Activity Page 14-6*.

• What does it mean to love someone? Where is love? Is it in our hearts? If we have *Brotherly love*, what would that mean? Do you have a brother or a sister? What do you want to do for them if they are hurt or sick? Do you want to take care of them? *Brotherly love* is internal. It will only be seen when we do something.

• When we do things for someone else, we are *caring* for them. *Caring* for others is external.

• What is character? What *character* did the Pilgrims show during the first winter in Plymouth? Did they only take

care of themselves and their family? Were they willing to take care of others? What was their attitude?

• Use *Student Activity Page 14-6*. Reason from the Student Text to make a list of the actions which demonstrated the *Brotherly love* and *Christian care* the Pilgrims showed for one another.

• Note how many of the Pilgrims died during the first winter. Historians tell us that every family had someone in their family die. At the teacher's discretion, additional information could be given concerning the burials during the first winter.

Due to uncertainty about the Indians, the Pilgrims hesitated to reveal the weakness of the colony. Consequently, they buried the dead at night, using a common grave, so the Indians would not realize how many had died.

A memorial has been erected in Plymouth on Burial Hill, listing the many who died the first winter and were buried there.

Cultivating Student Mastery

1. Name 2 or 3 ways you can show brotherly love and Christian care for others. At the bottom of the page, draw a picture of yourself showing Christian care of someone else.

Leading Idea

God's Providence in sending Samoset and Squanto

Student Text, pages 91-92

• Bradford wrote concerning Samoset's arrival in Plymouth: "All this while ye Indians came skulking about them, and

would sometimes show them selves aloofe of, but when any aproached near them, they would rune away. And once they stoale away their tools wher they had been at worke, & were gone to diner. But about ye 16. of March a certaine Indian came bouldly amongst them, and spoke to them in broken English, which they could well understand, but marvelled at it. At length they understood by discourse with him, that he was not of these parts, but belonged to ye eastrene parts, wher some English-ships came to fhish, with whom he was acquainted, & could name sundrie of them by their names, amongst whom he had gott his language. He became proftable to them in aquainting them with many things concerning ye state of ye cuntry . . . His name was Samaset; he tould them also of another Indian whos name was Squanto, a native of this place, who had been in England & could speake better English then him selfe. Being, after some time of entertainmente & gifts, dismist, a while after he came againe, & 5. more with him. & they brought againe all ye tooles that

were stolen away before, and made way for ye coming of their great Sachem, called Massasoyt; who, about 4. or 5. days after, came with the cheefe of his friends & other attendance, with the aforesaid Squanto. With whom, after frendly entertainment, & some gifts given him, they made a peace with him (which hath now continued this 24. years) in these terms."[34]

• At the time of Bradford's writing, the peace treaty between the colonists and Indians had lasted for 24 years. History reveals this peace actually lasted at least 50 years.

• Years before, Squanto had been captured by fishermen and taken to England. His knowledge of English was greater than that of the other Indians. God worked through Squanto to bring assistance to the Pilgrim colony. They, in turn, were able to share with him their faith in Christ.

For Reflection and Reasoning

• Review: What is Providence? How did God show His special care of the Pilgrims? Did they land at the place where they had planned? How can we know that it was the place that God had planned?

• Do you think the Pilgrims were surprised when Samoset spoke to them

in English? How does this show God's Providence?

• Reason with the students concerning the commitment of these Pilgrims — when the Mayflower went back to England, not one went back.

• Color the picture of Squanto and the Pilgrim boys, *Student Activity Page 14-7.*

Leading Idea

"America's heritage of Christian character" — brotherly love and Christian care

Student Text, pages 92-93

• The first two years in the Plymouth colony were extremely difficult. Yet, as new colonists arrived, they were wel-

comed. Many of the new arrivals came without adequate supplies and some with no supplies. The Pilgrims willingly shared their homes and small supply with the newcomers. This put a great strain on the colony's already limited food supply.

Bradford tells us that at one point they were reduced to "a quarter of a pound of bread a day to each person".

For Reflection and Reasoning

• Review: What is character? What does it mean to have brotherly love and Christian care? How did the Pilgrims show their brotherly love to the new colonists who arrived? What did it cost the Pilgrims?

• Review the chart illustrating the relationship of *Brotherly love* and *Chris-*

tian care. Reason from the Student Text concerning the Pilgrims' love and care for the newcomers.

• Read Matthew 22:36-40.

Cultivating Student Mastery

1. How did the Pilgrims show their brotherly love for the newcomers to the colony?

Leading Idea

Owning personal property makes all hands industrious

Student Text, pages 93-94

• For two years the Plymouth colony operated under the collective system established by the agreement of the London Company. All things were held in common and distributed equally. During that time, they continued to suffer from lack of food. They realized they must consider how they could raise as much corn as possible. Bradford related: "At length, after much debate of things, the Govr (with ye advise of ye cheefest amongest them) gave way that they should set corne every man for his owne perticuler, and in that regard trust to them selves; in all other things to goe on in ye generall way as before."[35]

The land was divided so that each family could raise their own crops. Bradford described the "good success" that resulted from this new system. Many were more willing to work, who had before made excuses. ". . . For it made all hands very industrious, so as much more corne was planted then other waise would have bene by any means ye Govr or any other could use, and saved him a great deall of trouble, and gave farr better contente."

Bradford expanded upon the injustice of collectivism, stating that "God in his wisdome saw another course fiter for them."[36]

For Reflection and Reasoning

• Why did the Pilgrims own everything together? What does it mean to "own

everything together?" Does your family own their own home? Do the neighbors own their own home? Who must take care of your home? Who must take care of the neighbor's house? Do you have things that belong to you — clothes, toys, etc.? Who is to take care of them?

What resulted in the Plymouth colony? Point out that the difficulties experienced were not because the Pilgrims had poor character but were caused by the system of ownership. How do we know it was not the problem of their character?

• Do you have your own doll, truck, bicycle or skateboard? Do you want anything to happen to it? What does it mean to be "responsible" for what you own? Will you be more concerned to care for *property* if it belongs only to you, or if it belongs to you and someone else?

• Have you ever planted your own garden — vegetables or flowers? Who is responsible to pull the weeds? Who is responsible to water the plants? Do you have more responsibility than if the garden belongs to the whole family?

Would the Pilgrims have felt more responsible when they owned their own field? Why?

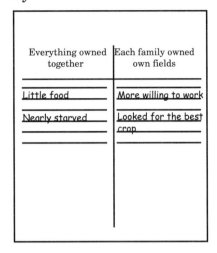

Everything owned together	Each family owned own fields
Little food	More willing to work
Nearly starved	Looked for the best crop

• *Student Activity Page 14-8.* Reasoning from the Student Text, develop a chart contrasting the results of owning property collectively and each family having their own fields.

Leading Idea

God's Providence in sending rain

Student Text, page 95

• In 1623, after laying aside collectivism, the colonists were still faced with the difficulties of the weather. Looking forward to the best crop Plymouth had ever had, they saw it threatened with a drought from May until July. They knew that God controls the weather, and turned to Him in a special day of prayer. God saw fit to send them a gentle rain. Bradford tells us "Upon which they sett a parte a solemne day of humilliation, to seek ye Lord by humble & fervente prayer, in this great distrese. And he was pleased to give them a gracious & speedy answer, both to their owne, & the Indeans admiration, that lived amongst them. For all ye morning, and greatest part of the day, it was clear weather & very hotte, and not a cloud or any signe of raine to be seen, yet toward evening it began to overcast, and shortly after to raine, with shuch sweete and gentle showers, as gave them cause of rejoyceing, & blesing God. . . Which did so apparently revive & quicken ye decayed corne & other fruits, as was wonderfull to see, and made ye Indeans astonished to behold: . . ."[37]

For Reflection and Reasoning

• Who controls the weather? Who sends the rain? The Pilgrims had done all they could do to have a good crop, but God must send the rain.

• Read verses that confirm God's control of the weather.

• Have students draw a picture of the gentle rain falling on a field of corn.

Cultivating Student Mastery

1. Who controls the weather?

2. How did God answer the Pilgrim's prayer?

Leading Idea

Praise him for his mighty acts.
Psalm 150:2

Student Text, pages 95-96

• Recognizing God's Hand in sending the rain and the great harvest of 1623, the Pilgrims set apart a day of thanks-giving. Future generations commemorated these events, remembering God's Hand of blessing in America.

For Reflection and Reasoning

• What does it mean to give thanks? Read selected verses which teach that we are to give thanks to God. Examples: Psalm 150:2; Psalm 100; Psalm 50:14; etc.

• Who sent the rain? Who had given the Pilgrims a good harvest? The Pilgrims knew that God had sent the rain. He was the one who had given them the good harvest.

• Sing songs of thanksgiving: *Come Ye Thankful People; America, the Beautiful; Faith of our Fathers; Great God of Nations; etc.*

• Does God send blessings in our lives? Should we thank Him for His blessings?

• *Student Activity Page 14-9.* Students list blessings for which they are thankful. Color the picture of the Pilgrims.

Leading Idea

God used the Pilgrims as stepping stones in the establishment of a self governing nation.

Student Text, page 96

• In conclusion, the Pilgrims did become the "stepping stones" for a greater work. The idea of self government, first in the life of the individual, then in the church, and then in civil government is the basis of the United States of America. This seed took 150 years to grow into a nation.

For Reflection and Reasoning

• What had the people learned in Plymouth concerning self-government? Did they need a king to govern them?

• Using *Student Activity Page 14-10*, review the result of God's Word in the heart of the individual and its effect in the church and civil government.

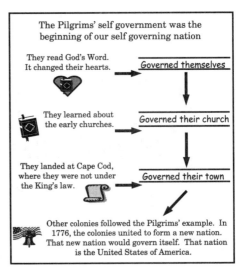

The Pilgrims' self government was the beginning of our self governing nation

They read God's Word. It changed their hearts. → Governed themselves

They learned about the early churches. → Governed their church

They landed at Cape Cod, where they were not under the King's law. → Governed their town

Other colonies followed the Pilgrims' example. In 1776, the colonies united to form a new nation. That new nation would govern itself. That nation is the United States of America.

Supplemental Activities

• Prepare a Mayflower Compact document for signing, using a paper which looks like parchment. Have students take turns signing the compact.

  Students may dress as Pilgrims or cut out paper collars. The students could put the collars over their regular school clothes.

• Plan a Thanksgiving celebration. Students may dress as Pilgrims or Indians. Plan authentic Pilgrim food.

PATRIOT
First Christian Republic
Chapters 15-17
4-5 Weeks

Chapter 15
One Nation Under God
2-3 Days

> **Leading Idea**
>
> *The world's first Christian Republic established upon Biblical principles of self and civil government*
>
> Student Text, page 97

• The Biblical idea of the individual governing his own actions, and the extension of that idea into church government and then civil government, first occurred in the small band of Pilgrims who settled Plymouth. These ideas were considered, written about, and internalized in each section of the nation. This took 150 years after the settling of Plymouth. The people of colonial America had learned to write their own constitutions and laws based upon the extension of individual self government into the civil government.

• Many people believed the colonists lacked education. However, "When the American State Papers arrived in Europe they surprised and astonished the 'enlightened men.' Americans had been dismissed as 'illiterate backwoodsmen' as, perhaps, 'law-defying revolutionists.' But when these papers were read they were found to contain 'nearly every quality indicative of personal and national greatness.'"[38]

Moses Coit Tyler

For Reflection and Reasoning

• Review: 1) Definition of government; 2) two spheres of government — internal and external. See Teacher's Guide, pages 21-22.

• Review the geographic concept of cities, states, and nations.

• Review the idea that *the individual is responsible for civil government,* see Teacher's Guide, page 26. If the people had learned to be self governed, what kind of civil government would they want? Would they want a king or people in England to make the laws for them? Why or why not?

• The span of 150 years, 1620-1770, will be difficult for students of this age to understand. Relate this amount of time to their family. How many generations would have lived in that 150 years?

• It may be helpful to look at a current map of the United States to identify the city and state where you live. Relate the size to the nation — the United States of America.

• The Student Text identifies that colonists had come from several different countries. Locate these countries on a map of Europe or a world map. If students are familiar with their family history, identify and locate the countries from which their ancestors came.

• Reason from the Student Text regarding how the colonists learned to govern themselves. See *Student Activity Page 15-1.*

One Nation Under God

Colonists learned to govern themselves

1. Made their own laws

2. Chose the people who would make the laws

• Begin outlining and labeling a map of the thirteen colonies, *Student Activity Page 15-2.* Optional: Use labeled map, *Student Activity Page 15-3.* Students outline the thirteen colonies.

Cultivating Student Mastery

1. Who made the laws for the American colonies?

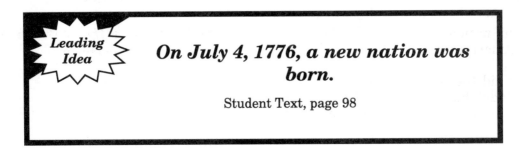

Leading Idea

On July 4, 1776, a new nation was born.

Student Text, page 98

• In 1776, representatives met together and voluntarily approved the Declara-

tion of Independence. "We, therefore, the Representatives of the UNITED

STATES OF AMERICA, in General Congress, Assembled, appealing to the Supreme Judge of the World for the Rectitude of our Intentions, do, in the Name, and by Authority of the good People of these Colonies, solemnly Publish and Declare, That these United Colonies are, and of Right ought to be, Free and Independent States: . . . And for the support of this Declaration, with a firm Reliance on the Protection of divine Providence, we mutually pledge to each other our Lives, our Fortunes, and our sacred Honor."

• The Representatives believed that, under the Divine authority, they had the right to declare themselves free and independent and to govern their own states with no further connection to Great Britain.

• "The day after the Declaration was made, Mr. [John] Adams, in writing to a friend, declared the event to be one that 'ought to be commemorated, as the day of deliverance, by solemn acts of devotion to God Almighty. It ought to be solemnized with pomp and parade, with shows, games, sports, guns, bells, bonfires, and illuminations, from one end of this continent to the other, from this time forward, for evermore.'

"And on the day of his death, hearing the noise of bells and cannon, he asked the occasion. On being reminded that it was 'Independent day,' he replied, 'Independence for ever!'"[39]

Daniel Webster,
The Works of Daniel Webster

Note: The Declaration of Independence will be studied in a later year.

For Reflection and Reasoning

• Why do you celebrate your birthday? Our nation has a birthday, too. July 4, 1776, is the date that the United States of America declared herself independent from England. This is the birthday of our nation.

• What is a "Declaration"? The men who signed the Declaration of Independence knew they could lose all they had, even their lives. Why were they willing to make such a choice?

Is it sometimes difficult to do what is right and what we know God wants us to do?

• If our nation was born in 1776, how old is America today?

• Why did the representatives that met in Philadelphia think that the colonies could form their own nation? The

teacher may choose to read selected statements from the Declaration regarding the representatives dependence upon God in making this decision.

• Show the students a copy of the Declaration of Independence.

• Name the 13 colonies which were part of the United States of America on July 4, 1776. Point out their location on the map, Student Text, page 97.

Suggested Student Notes

July 4, 1776

The birthday of the United States of America

Students may illustrate their page by drawing flags, fireworks, etc.

Supplemental Activities

Students would enjoy celebrating the birthday of the United States with a special birthday party. Such a celebration could include:

1. Songs
2. Poems celebrating the birth of the nation
3. A "Fourth of July" craft
4. A small parade around the classroom or school building, with students carrying flags and playing patriotic songs on kazoos, drums, etc.
5. A patriotic birthday cake

Chapter 16
George Washington
Father of our Country
9-11 Days

Leading Idea

God prepares individuals for His purpose — George Washington

Student Text, pages 99

• Webster defines *leader* as "One that leads or conducts; a guide; One who goes first."

• During the Colonial Period, God brought forth the leadership which was required to lead the new nation through the Revolutionary War and Constitutional Period. George Washington stands tall among that leadership.

Washington's love of learning and ability for self-education was evident as a young boy.

• ". . . George was yet in early childhood: as his intellect dawned he received the rudiments of education in the best establishment for the purpose that the neighborhood afforded. It was what was called, in popular parlance, an 'old field school-house;' humble enough in its pretensions, and kept by one of his father's tenants named Hobby, who, moreover was sexton of the parish. The instruction doled out by him must have been of the simplest kind, reading, writing, and ciphering, perhaps; but George had the benefit of mental and moral culture at home, from an excellent father. . . .

". . . The sudden and untimely death of his father, which took place on the 12th of April, 1743. . .

"George, now eleven years of age, . . . had been left under the guardianship of their mother . . . Endowed with plain, direct good sense, thorough conscientiousness, and prompt decision, she governed her family strictly, but kindly, exacting deference while she inspired affection. George . . . was thought to be her favorite, yet she never gave him undue preference, and the implicit deference exacted from him in childhood continued to be habitually observed by him to the day of her death. He inherited from her a high temper and a spirit of command, but her early precepts and example taught him to restrain and govern that temper, and to square his conduct on the exact principles of equity and justice.

"Tradition gives an interesting picture of the widow, with her little flock gathered round her, as was her daily wont, reading to them lessons of religion and morality out of some standard work. Her favorite volume was Sir Matthew Hale's Contemplations, moral and divine. The admirable maxims therein contained, for outward action as well as self-government, sank deep into the mind of George, and, doubtless, had a great influence in forming his character. They certainly were exemplified in his conduct throughout life. This mother's manual, bearing his mother's name, Mary Washington, written with her own hand, was ever preserved by him with filial care. . . A precious document! Let those who wish to know the moral foundation of his character consult its pages.

"Having no longer the benefit of a father's instructions at home, and the scope of tuition of Hobby, the sexton, being too limited for the growing wants of his pupil, George was now sent to reside with Augustine Washington, at Bridges Creek, and enjoy the benefit of a superior school in that neighborhood, kept by a Mr. Williams. His education, however, was plain and practical. He never attempted the learned languages, nor manifested any inclination for rhetoric or belles-lettres. His object, or the object of his friends, seems to have been confined to fitting him for ordinary business. His manuscript schoolbooks still exist, and are models of neatness and accuracy. . . .

"Above all, his inherent probity and the principles of justice on which he regulated all his conduct, even at this early period of life, were soon appreciated by his schoolmates; he was referred to as an umpire in their disputes, and his decisions were never reversed. . . . He was not legislator of the school; thus displaying in boyhood a type of the future man."[40]

Washington Irving,
Life of George Washington

For Reflection and Reasoning

• What is a *leader*? Do you play games which have a *leader*? Are there times when you stand in a line, and must follow the *leader*?

Who is the *leader* in your home? What would your home be like if there was not a *leader*?

Even as children need leaders, so a young nation needed strong leadership. God raised up leaders in America to guide the colonies through the difficult time of separation from England. George Washington was a great leader of that time.

• Set the historic stage of George Washington's birth. He was born when the thirteen colonies were English colonies. At the time of his birth, no efforts were being made to separate from England.

• See *Student Activity Page 16-1.* Students may record a simple definition of a leader: "One who goes first."

Washington's education had many facets. Reasoning from the Student Text, the students may list the things he learned. This page will be completed in a later lesson.

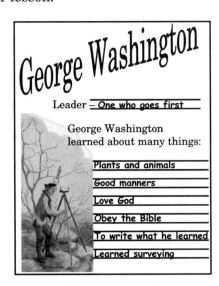

• Continue coloring and labeling the map of the thirteen colonies begun with Chapter 15. Allow adequate time during the study of George Washington to complete the map.

Leading Idea

God prepares individuals for His purpose — George Washington.

Student Text, page 100

• "To school, therefore, George returned, and continued his studies for nearly two years longer, devoting himself especially to mathematics, and accomplishing himself in those branches calculated to fit him either for civil or military service. Among these, one of the most important in the actual state of the country was land surveying. In this he schooled himself thoroughly, using the highest processes of the art; making surveys about the neighborhood, and keeping regular field books, some of which we have examined, in which the boundaries and measurements of the fields surveyed were carefully entered, and diagrams made, with a neatness and exactness as if the whole related to important land transactions instead of being mere school exercises. Thus, in his earliest days, there was perseverance and completeness in all his undertakings. Nothing was left half done, or done in a hurried and slovenly manner. The habit of mind thus cultivated continued throughout life; so that however complicated his tasks and overwhelming his cares, in the arduous and hazardous situations in which he was often placed, he found time to do everything, and to do it well. He had acquired the magic of method, which of itself works wonders."[41]

Washington Irving,
Life of George Washington

For Reflection and Reasoning

• Review: What is a leader? When was George Washington born? What did he learn as a young boy?

• What is diligence? How was Washington diligent in his learning? What record do we have of his learning?

• What is surveying? Note the picture of Washington on page 100. What is the instrument that Washington is using? Why is surveying important? How does it help to protect the land you own?

• How well did Washington learn surveying? How did Washington's education help him to be a surveyor? Why should you try to learn in school?

• How did Washington's work as a surveyor help him to learn about the country? Later, when he became the leader of the American army, how did this knowledge help him?

• What character was evident in Washington's life concerning learning? Did it seem that he valued learning? How did this help him to be a "leader"?

• What is responsibility? Responsibility can be given to people who are diligent and have good self government.

• Complete *Student Activity Page 16-1.* Record "To write what he learned" and "Learned surveying."

Leading Idea

As a young man, Washington was asked to carry out an official and dangerous mission.

Student Text, page 101

• George Washington's first official mission was as emissary for the Governor of Virginia to the Commandant of the French Forces on the Ohio, October 1753-January, 1754. He recorded the events of this journey in his journal:

October, 1753. *"Wednesday, 31st.* I was commissioned and appointed by the Honourable *Robert Dinwiddie, Esq:* Governor, &c., of *Virginia,* to visit and deliver a letter to the Commandant of the *French* forces on the *Ohio,* and set out on the intended Journey the same day: The next I arrived at *Fredericksburg,* and engaged Mr. *Jacob Vanbraam,* to be my *French* interpreter; and proceeded with him to *Alexandria,* where we provided Necessaries. From thence we went to *Winchester,* and got Baggage, Horses, &c; and from thence we pursued the new Road to *Wills-Creek,* where we arrived the 14th of *November.*

"Here I engaged Mr. *Gist* to pilot us and also hired four others as Servitors, *Barnaby Currin* and *John Mac-Quire,* Indian Traders, *Henry Steward,* and *William Jenkins;* and in company with those persons left the Inhabitants the Day following.

"The excessive Rains and vast Quantity of Snow which had fallen, prevented our reaching Mr. *Frazier's,* an Indian Trader, at the Mouth of *Turtle Creek,* on *Monongahela,* till Thursday, the 22d. . . .

"The Waters were quite impassible without swimming our Horses; which obliged us to get the Loan of a Canoe from *Frazier,* . . .

"As soon as I came into Town, I went to *Monakatoocha* . . . and informed him by . . . my *Indian* Interpreter, that I was sent a Messenger to the *French* General; and was ordered to call upon the Sachems of the *Six Nations,* to acquaint them with it. . . I invited him and the other great Men present to my Tent, where they stayed about an Hour and return'd. . .

"25th. Came to Town four or ten *Frenchmen* who had deserted from a Company at the *Kuskuskas,* which lies at the Mouth of this River. . .

"I enquired into the Situation of the *French,* on the *Mississippi,* their Number, and what Forts they had built. . .

"About 3 o'Clock this Evening the Half-King came to Town. I went up and invited him . . privately to my Tent; and desir'd him to relate some of the particulars of his Journey to the French *Commandant,* and Reception there: Also to give me an account of the Ways and Distance . . .

"26th. . . . As I had Orders to make all possible Dispatch, and waiting here was very contrary to my Inclinations, I thanked him in the most suitable Manner I could; and told him, that my Business required the greatest Expedition, and would not admit of that Delay. He was not well pleased that I should offer to go before the Time he had appointed, and told me, that he could not consent to our going without a Guard, for fear some Accident should befal us and draw a Reflection upon him. . . . As I found it was impossible to get-off without affronting them in the most egregious Manner, I consented to stay. . .

"30th. Last Night the great Men assembled to their Council-House, to consult further about this Journey, and who were to go: The Result of which was, that only three of their Chiefs, with one of their best Hunters, should be our Convoy. The Reason they gave for not send-

ing more, after what had been proposed at Council the 26th, was that a greater Number might give the *French* Suspicions of some bad Design, and cause them to be treated rudely: But I rather think they could not get their Hunters in.

December "[*4th*] . . . We found the *French* Colours hoisted at a House from which they had driven Mr. *John Frazier,* an *English* Subject. I immediately repaired to it . . . They told me, That it was their absolute Design to take Possession of the *Ohio,* and . . . they would do it; For that altho' they were sensible the *English* could raise two Men for their one; yet they knew their Motions were too slow and dilatory to prevent any Undertaking of theirs. They pretend to have an undoubted Right to the River, from a Discovery made by one *La Salle* 60 Years ago; and the Rise of this Expedition is, to prevent our settling on the River or Waters of it, as they had heard of some Families moving-out in Order thereto. . . .

"13*th*. The chief Officers retired, to hold a Council of War; which gave me an Opportunity of taking the Dimensions of the Fort, and making what Observations I could. . .

"I could get no certain account of the Number of Men here: But according to the best Judgment I could form, there are an Hundred exclusive of Officers, of which there are many. I also gave Orders to the People who were with me, to take an exact Account of the Canoes which were hauled-up to convey their Forces down in the Spring. This they did. . .

"14*th*. As the Snow increased very fast, and our Horses daily became weaker, I sent them off unloaded; . . . To make all convenient Dispatch to *Venango,* and there await our Arrival, if there was a prospect of the Rivers freezing: If not, then to continue down to *Shanapin's* Town, at the Forks of the *Ohio,* and there to wait till we came to cross the *Aliganey;* intending myself to go down by Water, as I had the Offer of a Canoe or two.

"As I found many Plots concerted to retard the *Indians* Business, and prevent their returning with me: I endeavor'd all that lay in my Power to frustrate their

Schemes, and to hurry them on to execute their intended Design. They accordingly pressed for Admittance this Evening, which at Length was granted them, privately, with the Commander and one or two other officers. The Half-King told me, that he offer'd the Wampum to the Commander, who evaded taking it, and made many fair Promises of Love and Friendship; said he wanted to live in Peace, and trade amicably with them, as a Proof of which he would send some Goods down immediately to the *Logg's-*Town for them. But I rather think the Design of that is, to bring away all our straggling Traders they meet with, as I privately understood they intended to carry an Officer, &c, with them. And what rather confirms this Opinion, I was enquiring of the Commander, by what Authority he had made Prisoners of several of our *English* Subjects. He told me that the Country belong'd to them; that no *Englishman* had a Right to trade upon those Waters; and that he had Orders to make every Person Prisoner who attempted it on the *Ohio,* or the Waters of it.

"15*th*. The Commandant ordered a plentiful Store . . . to be put on Board our Canoe; and appeared to be extremely complaisant, though he was exerting every Artifice which he could invent to set our own *Indians* at Variance with us, to prevent their going 'till after our Departure. Presents, Rewards, and every Thing which could be suggested by him or his Officers. — I can't say that ever in my Life I suffered so much Anxiety as I did in this Affair: I saw that every Stratagem which the most fruitful Brain could invent, was practised, to win the Half-King to their Interest; and that leaving him here was giving them the Opportunity they aimed at. — I went to the Half-King and press'd him in the strongest Terms to go: He told me the Commandant would not discharge him 'till the Morning. I then went to the Commandant, and desired him to do their Business; and complain'd of ill Treatment: For keeping them, as they were Part of my Company, was detaining me. This he promised not to do, but to forward my

Journey as much as he could. He protested he did not keep them, but was ignorant of the Cause of their Stay; though I soon found it out: — He had promised them, a present of Guns, &c, if they would wait 'till the morning.

"As I was very much press'd by the *Indians*, to wait this Day for them, I consented, on a Promise, That nothing should hinder them in the Morning.

"16*th*. The *French* were not slack in their Inventions to keep the *Indians* this Day also: But as they were obligated, according to Promise, to give the Present, they then endeavored to try the Power of Liquor; which I doubt not would have prevailed at any other Time than this; But I urged and insisted with the King so closely upon his Word, that he refrained, and set off with us as he had engaged.

"We had a tedious and very fatiguing Passage down the Creek. Several Times we were like to have been staved against Rocks; and many Times were obliged all Hands to get out and remain in the Water Half an Hour or more, getting over the Shoals. At one Place the Ice had lodged and made it impassable by Water; therefore we were obliged to carry our Canoe across a Neck of Land, a quarter of a Mile over. We did not reach *Venango*, till the 22d, where we met with our Horses. . . .

"23*d*. . . . Our Horses were now so weak and feeble, and the Baggage so heavy . . . that we doubted much their performing it; therefore myself and others . . . gave up our Horses for Packs, to assist along with the Baggage. I put myself in an *Indian* walking Dress,[42] and continued with them three Days, till I found there was no Probability of their getting home in any reasonable Time. The Horses grew less able to travel every Day; the Cold increased very fast; and the Roads were becoming much worse by a deep Snow, continually freezing: Therefore as I was uneasy to get back, to make Report of my Proceedings to his Honour, the Governor, I determined to prosecute my Journey the nearest Way through the Woods, on Foot. . . .

"I took my necessary Papers; pulled off my Cloaths; and tied myself up in a Match Coat.[43] Then with Gun in Hand and Pack at my Back, in which were my Papers and Provisions, I set-out with Mr. *Gist*, fitted in the same Manner, on *Wednesday*, the 26th.

"The Day following, just after we had passed a Place called the *Murdering-Town* . . . we fell in with a Party of *French* Indians, who had lain in Wait for us. One of them fired at Mr. *Gist* or me, not 15 steps off, but fortunately missed. . . . . The next Day we continued travelling till quite dark, and got to the River . . . We expected to have found the River frozen, but it was not, only about 50 Yards from each Shore; The Ice I suppose had broken up above, for it was driving in vast Quantities.

"There was no way for getting over but on a Raft; Which we set about with but one poor Hatchet, and finished just after Sun-setting. This was a whole Day's Work. Then set off; But before we were Half Way over, we were jammed in the Ice, in such a Manner that we expected every Moment our Raft to sink, and ourselves to perish. I put-out my setting Pole to try to stop the Raft, that the Ice might pass by; when the Rapidity of the Stream threw it with so much Violence against the Pole, that it jerked me out into ten Feet Water: but I fortunately saved myself by catching hold of one of the Raft Logs. Notwithstanding all our efforts we could not get the Raft to either Shore; but were obliged, as were near an Island to quit our Raft, and make to it.

"The Cold was so extremely severe, that Mr. *Gist* had all his Fingers, and some of his Toes frozen; but the water was shut up so hard, that we found no Difficulty in getting-off the Island, on the Ice, in the Morning. . .

January, 1754 "*Tuesday, the* 1st *Day of January,* we left Mr. *Frazier's* House, and arrived at Mr. *Gist's* at *Monongahela* the 2d, where I bought a Horse, Saddle, etc; the 6th we met 17 Horses loaded with Materials and Stores, for Fort at the Forks of *Ohio*, and the Day after some Families going out to settle: This Day we arrived at *Wills* Creek, after as fatiguing a Journey as it is possible to conceive, rendered so by excessive bad Weather.

From the first Day of December to the 15th, there was but one Day on which it did not rain or snow incessantly: and throughout the whole Journey we met with nothing but one continued Series of cold wet Weather, which occasioned very uncomfortable Lodgings: especially after we had quitted our Tent, which was some Screen from the Inclemency of it.

"On the 11*th* I got to Belvoir: where I stopped one Day to take necessary Rest; and then set out and arrived in Williamsburg the 16th; when I waited upon his Honour the Governor with the Letter I had brought from the French Commandant; and to give an Account of the Success of my Proceedings. This I beg leave to do by offering the foregoing Narrative as it contains the most remarkable Occurrences which happened in my Journey."[44]

For Reflection and Reasoning

• Review the relationship of the colonies to England.

• On a map, locate Williamsburg, Virginia and consider the path of his journey. Washington left from Williamsburg, traveling across Pennsylvania. He crossed the forks of the Monongahalla, Allegheny, and Ohio Rivers. From there, he went up to Fort LeBoeuf, near Lake Erie.

• How important was the journey that Washington made to the French commander in the Ohio Valley? Who asked Washington to make the journey? How old was he? What does this identify about Washington's character, that he was given such a responsible job at such a young age?

• The founders of our nation were remarkable for keeping journals. Washington's journal reflects great attention to detail and recognition of Providence.

• Few details of the mission are included in the Student Text. Using the resource from Washington's Diary, the teacher may expand the details, as appropriate.

• Consider: What made the journey so difficult? The Student Text identifies the natural elements which Washington faced. What other enemies did he face? *Note evidence of Washington's wisdom at the French fort. Considering Washington's age, what is remarkable about his character?*

Cultivating Student Mastery

1. How do we know about many things from Washington's life?

2. How was Washington prepared to carry out the mission for the Governor of Virginia?

God protected George Washington during the French and Indian War.

Student Text, page 102

• George Washington was protected during the battle in which General Braddock was killed. Washington received four bullet holes in his coat. The following letters of Washington record details of this event:

• Letter to Robert Dinwiddie, July 18, 1755: "As I am favoured with an opportunity, I should think myself inexcusable, was I to omit giving you some account of our late Engagement with the French on the Monongahela the 9th Inst.

"We continued our March for Fort Cumberland to Frazer's (which is within 7 Miles of Duquisne) without meeting any extraordinary event, having only a straggler or two picked Up by the French Indians. When we came to this place, we were attacked, (very unexpectedly) by about 300 French and Indians; Our number's consisted of about 1300 well armed Men, chiefly regulars, who were immediately struck with such Panick, that nothing but confusion and disobedience of order's prevailed amongst them: The Officers in general behaved with incomparable bravery, for which they greatly suffered, there being near 60 killed and wounded A large Proportion out of the number we had! The Virginians behaved like Men, and died like Soldier's; for I believe out of 3 Companies that were on the ground that Day, scarce 30 were left alive: Captain Peyrouny and all his Officers down to a Corporal, were killed; Captain Polson shared almost as hard a Fate, for only one of his Escaped: In short the dastardly behaviour of the Regular Troops exposed all those who were inclined to do their duty, to almost certain Death; and at length, in despite of every effort to the contrary, broke & run as Sheep before Hounds, leaving the Artillery, Ammunition, Provision, Baggage & in short every thing a prey to the Enemy; and when we endeavoured to rally them

in hopes of regaining the ground and what we had left upon it, it was with as little success as if we had attempted to have stopped the wild Bears of the Mountains or rivulets with our feet, for they would break by in spite of every effort that could be made to prevent it.

"The General was wounded in the Shoulder, & the Breast; of which he died three days after; his two Aids de Camp were both wounded, but are in a fair way of Recovering; . . . It is supposed that we had 300 or more killed; about that number we brought off wounded; and it is conjectured (I believe with much truth) that two thirds of both received their shot from our own cowardly Regulars, who gathered themselves into a body contrary to orders 10 or 12 deep, would then level, Fire, & shoot down the Men before them. . . ."[45]

• Letter to John Augustine Washington, July 18, 1755: "As I have heard since my arrival at this place, a circumstantial account of my death and dying Speech, I take this early opportunity of contradicting the first, and of assuring you that I have not, as yet, composed the latter. But by the all powerful dispensations of Providence, I have been protected beyond all human probability and expectation for I had 4 Bullets through my Coat, and two Horses shot under me yet escaped unhurt although death was levelling my companions on every side of me.

"We have been most scandalously beaten by a trifling body of men; but fatigue, and the want of time will prevent me from giving you any of the details untill I have the happiness of seeing you at Mount Vernon. . ."[46]

For Reflection and Reasoning

• Why is the war between France and England called the French and Indian War? By the time Washington was 23

years of age, he was an officer in the English army.

• How did the English soldiers plan to carry on a battle? Although not identified in the Student Text, how did the Indians fight? Why did this create a disaster for the English soldiers? How did the English soldier's red coats help the Indians?

• Washington's letters tell some of the difficulties of the battle. The teacher may expand as appropriate.

• *Student Activity Page 16-2.* Read excerpt from Washington's letter to his brother, John Augustine Washington, concerning God's protection of him during the battle. Student's record at the top: "God protected George Washington during the French and Indian War."

Then, guide the students in preparing a statement identifying God's Providence in the protection of George Washington during this battle. Consider why Washington was protected. Record the statement.

Leading Idea

No taxation without representation

Student Text, page 103

• Following the French and Indian War, England began to impose taxes on the American colonists to pay the expenses of the war. The American colonists were willing to pay the taxes, but only if they would have representation in the Parliament. They simply asked for the same representation as received by English subjects. England refused. A series of taxes were imposed, which the Americans refused to pay. *Further details of these events will be studied in a later year.*

• Webster defines a *tax* as "A rate or sum of money assessed on the person or property of a citizen by government, for the use of the nation or state."

• Webster defines *represent* as "To supply the place of; to act as a substitute for another" or "To stand in the place of."

• The population of the American colonies had grown to large numbers, in relation to the size and population of England. There were those in England who thought the colonies would eventually control England, rather than England controlling the colonies. Yet, the colonies had been extremely profitable financially for England.

There were those in England who recognized the validity of the colonists requests, and endeavored to educate others. They were not heard. See Edmund Burke's, *Conciliation with the Colonies.*

For Reflection and Reasoning

• What is a tax? When you purchase an item at the store, how do you know how much to pay? When you actually pay for the item, you usually pay some additional money beyond the price. That is a tax. Americans pay taxes in many ways.

What is the purpose of taxes?

Taxes have been collected for centuries. Consider Luke 2. Why did Mary and Joseph travel to Bethlehem?

• What is a representative? When are you the representative of another? When do you represent your parents? Are you ever a representative for your class? How are Christians representatives of Christ? Students may record a simple definition of represent.

● In the years following the French and Indian War, England began to tax the American colonists. The colonists were willing to pay taxes, but they asked for a representative.

Why was it important for the colonists to be represented in the Parliament? Were they asking for something unusual under English law?

● Why did England not want to allow representation of the colonies?

● Review: What was the Declaration of Independence?

● British troops had already been sent to the colonies. When the Americans declared independence, they knew they must prepare for war. To whom did they turn for leadership of the army? Why?

Suggested Student Notes

Represent—To stand in the place of another

Leading Idea

Though facing a great power, Washington trusted in God to lead in the battle.

Student Text, pages 103-104

● Throughout the ages, we see God's overruling Hand in the events of history. Certainly from man's view, the English army was much better prepared, experienced and equipped for war. However, God, in His wisdom, gave the eventual victory to the colonists.

● That difficult winter is described as follows: "Washington's army encamped at Whitemarsh, in a beautiful valley about fourteen miles from Philadelphia, where he remained until Dec. 11, 1777, and proceeded with his half-clad, half-barefooted soldiers to Valley Forge, about twenty miles northward from Philadelphia. These numbered about eleven thousand men, of whom not more than seven thousand were fit for field duty. The place was chosen because it was further from the danger of sudden attacks from the foe, and where he might more easily afford protection for the Congress sitting at York. Blood-stains, made by the lacerated feet of his barefooted soldiers, marked the line of their march to Valley Forge. There, upon the slopes of a narrow valley on the borders of the winding Schuylkill, they were encamped, with no shelter but rude log huts which they built themselves. The winter that ensued was severe. The soldiers shivered with cold and starved with hunger, and there their genuine patriotism was fully tested . . ."[47]
Benson J. Lossing
Cyclopædia of United States History

● "In this hour of darkness and of danger, when 'foes were strong and friends were few,' when every human prospect presented to the commander at Valley Forge was disheartening, he retires to a sequestered spot, and there laid the cause of his bleeding country at THE THRONE OF GRACE. That country had appealed in vain to the justice of her acknowledged sovereign; HE pleads her cause before the King of kings. . . . He sought to link our cause, by a sincere devotion, to the immutable throne of justice; to find wisdom to guide his own action; to place the

136

country in the RIGHT, so that he might bring upon her prosperity, as the natural result of justice to the injured."[48]

The Family Circle-1847

• "Trappe, Pennsylvania, May 7, 1778. I heard a find example today, namely, that His Excellency General Washington rode around among his army yesterday and admonished each and everyone to fear God, to put away the wickedness that has set in and become so general, and to practice the Christian virtues. From all ap-pearances this gentleman does not belong to the so-called world of society, for he respects God's Word, believes in the atonement through Christ, and bears himself in humility and gentleness. Therefore the Lord God has also singularly, yea, marvelously, preserved him from harm in the midst of countless perils, ambuscades, fatigues, etc. and has hitherto graciously held him in his hand as a chosen vessel."[49]

Rev. Henry Melchior Muhlenberg

For Reflection and Reasoning

• Review: Why were the Americans going to war?

• See *Student Activity Page 16-3.* Reason from the Student Text to complete a contrast between the English and American soldiers.

• Review: Who controls history?

• Locate Valley Forge on a map.

• There were many battles of the Revolutionary War. Further study of the War will be included in future years. One of the most difficult times for the American army was the winter of 1777. Using the additional information included in the Teacher's Guide, as appropriate, you may expand the details of that winter. Many descriptions include the poor soldiers, with clothes tattered, many with no shoes, facing the cold winter weather. Their hope could not be in the Congress, who was finding it difficult to provide them with provisions, but in the God who controls in the lives of men and nations.

• Guide the students in preparing a sentence which identifies Washington's dependence upon God during the Revolutionary War. Record the statement on the *Student Activity Page 16-3.*

Leading Idea

"Man proposes, God disposes."

Student Text, page 105

• The Battle of Yorktown proved a decisive battle in the Revolution. "Cornwallis despairing of aid from Clinton, and perceiving his strong fortifications crumbling, one by one, under the terrible storm of iron from a hundred heavy cannons, attempted to escape on the *night of the 16th.,* by crossing to Gloucester, breaking through the French troops stationed there, and making forced marches toward New York. When the van of his troops embarked, the waters of the York River were perfectly calm although dark clouds were gathering on the horizon. Then a storm arose as sudden and fearful as a summer tornado, dispersed the boats, compelled many to put back, and the attempt was abandoned. Hope now faded; and on the 19th., Cornwallis surrendered the posts at York Town and Gloucester, with almost seven thousand British soldiers, and his shipping and seamen, into the hands of Washington and DeGrasse."[50]

Benson J. Lossing,
History of the United States

For Reflection and Reasoning

• Locate Yorktown and the York River on a map.

• The last major battle of the Revolutionary War was fought at Yorktown. The American and French troops outnumbered Cornwallis. Without help from other British troops, he realized he should move the battle to a different location. He made his plans to cross the York River. How did God control who would win the battle? The Student Text does not express the drama of this storm. When they began their short voyage, the waters were calm. The York River is not a large river. Yet, the storm arose quickly — historians say it arose suddenly and fearfully. Why could the British soldiers not stay in their boats? What would have happened to them?

• Read Matthew 8:23-27. Who controls the winds and the waves?

• Although there were some small skirmishes after Yorktown, this battle essentially ended the War. What is a peace treaty? What does it mean to have peace with another nation?

• How did the British soldiers show Washington that they knew the war was over? How long had it been since the Declaration of Independence?

• What did the American soldiers do after the war?

• What did Washington do? What was Washington's hope? Although Washington wanted to enjoy life at Mount Vernon, God had prepared him for, yet, another task.

Suggested Student Notes

Cornwallis made his plans for the Battle at Yorktown. But God controlled the battle.

Cultivating Student Mastery

1. How did God control who won the Battle at Yorktown?

Leading Idea

The first constitutional republic was formed.

Student Text, page 105

• The Declaration of Independence had made each of the thirteen colonies a *free and independent state*. This resulted in many difficulties during the Revolutionary War. There was no authority given for the Congress to raise any taxes to pay for the War. Little money was available for food or supplies for the soldiers. These would arrive only as one of the states voluntarily chose to send financial support.

• The American colonies had many resources to trade with other nations. Was each state to work out their own relationship with other nations?

• The idea of a national government had long been discussed and would become a reality in 1787. As the Constitutional Convention met in Philadelphia that hot summer, the representatives brought forth a unique form of government. It was a Republic, built upon the idea that men could govern themselves.

The idea of local self government had been reasoned through and practiced since the landing of the Pilgrims in 1620. After 167 years, the world's first Christian Republic was established. There were thirteen colonies, but one nation under God.

For Reflection and Reasoning

• Review: What is a representative?

• Review: What is civil government?

• With the Declaration of Independence, the colonies had declared themselves "free and independent states." Look at the map of the thirteen colonies.

• If each state was "free and independent," there was not one nation. How could that be a problem? Were there thirteen countries? How would they trade with other nations? Would each state work by itself?

• The colonists realized that the thirteen states needed to work together as *one nation.* They recognized that there must be civil government for the entire nation.

• In 1787, there was a meeting in Philadelphia — this meeting was called the Constitutional Convention. The representatives of the thirteen states wrote a Constitution. This Constitution was to govern all thirteen states.

• Review: What is a law?

• Who was to make the laws for all of the states? How were these representatives chosen?

• See *Student Activity Page 16-4.* Students may record the date of the Constitution—1787— and Student Notes on activity page.

Suggested Student Notes

**Representatives from the 13 states
wrote the Constitution.**

Leading Idea

George Washington represented the people as the first President.

Student Text, pages 106-107

• The Constitution established the executive branch of the government, in the person of a President. George Washington, who had served the people well as Commander-in-Chief during the Revolutionary War and as President of the Constitutional Convention, was now chosen unanimously as the first President of the United States of America. John Adams was elected as the Vice President.

• Many challenges confronted Washington as the first President. His character as the leader of a free people consistently upheld the principles of liberty upon which the nation had been founded. God had prepared him to guide a new nation through its early difficulties. One of his great concerns was that the ideas of liberty and self government would be maintained in the new nation.

For Reflection and Reasoning

• What is a President? Who is the current President of the United States?

• Can the President do anything he wants in a nation? What protects the people against that idea?

• The Constitution expected the people to govern themselves. What type of government is that?

• See *Student Activity Page 16-5.* Students may record the Student Notes on the activity page. Reason from the Student Text to answer the question. The final statement will be recorded in the following lesson.

George Washington Father of our Country

George Washington was the first President of the United States.

What ideas did Washington want to always be part of the nation?

Liberty

Self government

First in war, first in peace, and first in the hearts of his countrymen.

Suggested Student Notes

George Washington was the first President of the United States.

Leading Idea

George Washington: "First in war, first in peace, and first in the hearts of his countrymen."

Student Text, pages 107-108

• Locate Virginia on a map of the United States. Locate Mount Vernon. What river does Mount Vernon face?

• Washington always enjoyed his time at Mount Vernon. His love for his country came before his love for Mount Vernon. How do we know this is true? He longed to be at Mount Vernon, but answered the call of duty to his nation many times.

• Review with the students the many responsibilities for the nation which Washington had taken. Why would it have been said that George Washington was "First in War, first in peace, and first in the hearts of his countrymen."

• Complete *Student Activity Page 16-5.* Using the Student Text, students may record the statement about George Washington.

Chapter 17
Daniel Boone
God's Man for Opening the Western Frontier

8-10 Days

Leading Idea

The Western lands were a new frontier.

Student Text, pages 109-110

• As God prepared a young man in Virginia to lead the young Republic, so he was simultaneously preparing a young man to open the Western frontier. The demands of the frontier held many unique challenges.

For Reflection and Reasoning

• What are colonial times?

• On a map, identify the many cities along the East coast of the thirteen colonies. Where were the major cities? Note the great expanse of land to the west.

• As the colonists arrived in America, how did they prepare the land so that cities could be built? What does it mean to *clear* the land?

• What is a frontier?

• Reasoning from the Student Text, prepare a contrast of life in the Eastern towns and life on the Western frontier. Students may record the conclusions on

Student Activity Page 17-1. Space is included for the students to draw pictures illustrating the contrast.

Eastern Towns	Western Frontier
Houses	Trees
Towns	Wild Animals
Farms	Few Forts

Opening the frontier demanded an individual with unique character.

Student Text, page 110

• In each epoch of history, the individuals who would open the door to new lands possessed unique character.

Paul was called to move the Gospel to Europe. He was God's man for that epoch of history.

John Wycliffe and William Tyndale were the individuals God used to make the Bible available to the individual in England.

Christopher Columbus was uniquely prepared to sail the vast Western Ocean and open the door to the New World.

The Pilgrims, studying the Word of God, had realized the need for personal, individual reformation. Recognizing Biblical principles of government relating to their church, they separated from the Church of England. In God's Providence, they arrived at Cape Cod, necessitating their immediate application of Biblical principles in the sphere of civil government. This small band became the seed of a new nation.

And, it would take a unique character to face the dangers of the Western frontier. God prepared Daniel Boone to be the man who would open the frontier for the westward movement in America.

For Reflection and Reasoning

• What would be difficult about exploring the Western frontier?

• What strengths did a man need in order to explore the Western frontier? Reason with the students to compile a list:
  • Friend to the Indians
  • Protect himself from wild animals
  • Find his own food
  • Take care of himself

This list, or selected points, could be included as Student Notes.

• How would a pathway to the frontier be helpful?

God prepared Daniel Boone to unlock the Western frontier.

Student Text, pages 110-111

• "He was Quaker-bred . . . A sweeter soul than his we shall not find though we search all the pages of history. Meeting every species of danger, he remained undaunted. Meeting every manner of adversity, he remained unsoured. With every reason for conceit, he remained unbitten of any personal vanity. To the end of his life it was his belief that he was 'an instrument ordained by Providence to settle the wilderness;' yet he lost no time in posing himself in any supposititious sainthood. Nor must we imagine him crude or ignorant in his simplicity, for those who knew him best state that he was 'a man of ambition, shrewdness and energy, as well as of fine social qualities and an extreme sagacity.'"[51]

Emerson Hough, *The Way to the West*

For Reflection and Reasoning

• When was Washington born? When was Daniel Boone born? How old was Washington when Boone was born?

• Locate Pennsylvania and North Carolina on a map.

• How would Boone's knowing the habits of animals help him to explore the wilderness? Would it help to protect him? How?

• How would you collect furs? What are the Eastern settlements?

• See *Student Activity Page 17-2*. Reasoning from the Student Text, answer the question, "How was Boone prepared to explore the wilderness?"

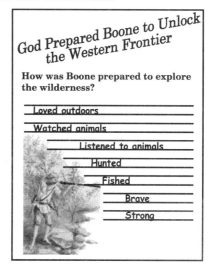

God Prepared Boone to Unlock the Western Frontier

How was Boone prepared to explore the wilderness?

Loved outdoors
Watched animals
Listened to animals
Hunted
Fished
Brave
Strong

> Leading Idea
>
> ## God prepared Daniel Boone to unlock the Western frontier.
>
> Student Text, pages 111-112

• "Previously to his marriage Boone had been a hunter, — what we would now call a professional hunter. He sometimes took hides and furs to the more distant Eastern settlements, and so saw some of the Virginia towns. He was, however, not merely a half-savage woods wanderer, although a past master in all woodcraft. The year before his marriage he was with the Pennsylvania militia, who fought the Indians along the border after the French had defeated George Washington and his Virginians at Great Meadows. In the fatal Braddock fight Daniel Boone was a wagoner in the baggage train, and barely escaped with his life in the panic flight."[52]

Emerson Hough, *The Way to the West*

For Reflection and Reasoning

• Review: What was the French and Indian War? What is the militia?

• John Finley spoke of the west. How did this influence Daniel Boone's future?

• Why would Boone enjoy traveling in woods which were full of wild animals?

• What is a log cabin? The students might enjoy building a cabin from Lincoln logs or Legos.

Leading Idea

God's Providence in Boone's first explorations of Kentucky

Student Text, pages 112-113

• "The journey over the mountains was not rapid and not continuous, it being necessary for the party to hunt as well as to explore. The rifle, the ax, the horse, the boat, were their aids and agents, their argument and answer to the wilderness. . .

"Boone and his friends seem to have camped on the east side of the Cumberland Mountains, where they remained for 'some days.' It was from this camp that they made expeditions, and at length climbed to a certain ridge whence they could see the glorious realm of Kentucky. On this day they saw their first herd of buffalo, the first trail-makers over the Appalachians, of which they killed some numbers. . . . Boone was delighted. There thrilled in his heart all the joy of the hunter and explorer. Now the little party moved over to the Red River, where Finley had formerly been located. 'Here,' said Boone, 'both man and beast may grow to their full size.' That was good American prophecy.

"For six months this adventurous little party lived and hunted in their new empire. Then, swiftly and without warning, there came a taste of some of the disadvantages of this wild residence. Stewart and Boone were taken captive by the Indians and were carried to the north, a march of seven days. On the seventh night they made their escape and came back to their bivouac on the Red River, only to find that their friends had left them and returned to the settlements."[53]

Emerson Hough, *The Way to the West*

For Reflection and Reasoning

• Locate Kentucky and the Cumberland Mountains on the map.

• What tools did an explorer need in the frontier? How might he use each tool?

• What wild animals did explorer's find in Kentucky? Which one did they see for the first time? Consider the picture in the Student Text. What animals can the students find in the picture?

If the students are not familiar with elk, deer, and buffalo, they might do some simple research about one of the animals.

• What idea did the men have about Kentucky?

• During their first exploration of Kentucky, what difficulties were encountered? Did this discourage them?

• How can you see God's Hand in their explorations? Consider their escape from the Indians, and their meeting with Squire Boone. How difficult would it have been for Squire Boone to have found them in the wilderness?

Cultivating Student Mastery

1. How might Boone and his companions have seen God's Hand of protection in their first explorations?

Leading Idea

Courage was demanded of Daniel Boone.

Student Text, page 114

• Webster defines courage as "Bravery. . . That quality of mind which enables men to encounter danger and difficulties with firmness, or without fear or depression of spirits; valor; boldness."

• "It is now that for the first time we may accord justice to the picture that shows us the pioneer, Daniel Boone, alone in the wilderness of Kentucky. He was at this time, so far as he knew, the only white man in that entire section of country. Fearless, adventurous and self-reliant, he extended his wanderings father to the west, and visited the site of what is now the city of Louisville. His life depended entirely upon his own vigilance. He was without bread or salt, without even a dog to keep him company or serve as guard. . . .

"He seems to have been happy, alone in a solitude whose nature one can not understand who had never found himself under conditions at least mildly similar. . . . 'He stood upon an eminence, whence, looking about in astonishment, he beheld the ample plain and beauteous upland, and saw the river rolling in silent dignity. The chirp of the birds solaced his cares with music. The numerous deer and elk which passed him gave him assurance that he was in the midst of plenty. Cheerfulness possessed his mind. He was a second Adam—if the figure be not too strong—giving names to springs and rivers and places all unknown to civilized man.' Such was the kingdom of the West."[54]

Emerson Hough, *The Way to the West*

For Reflection and Reasoning

• Define *courage* for the students. A simple definition might be, "Brave. Able to face danger without fear."

• What is fear? How do you face danger without being afraid? Have you ever been afraid?

• Read Deuteronomy 31:6. Is God always with us? If we know God is with us, will it help us have courage and not be afraid?

• Daniel Boone knew that God wanted him to explore the Western frontier. Might this have helped him to have courage and not to be afraid?

• How do we know that Daniel Boone had courage?

• Reason with the students to compile a list illustrating Daniel Boone's courage.
  • Did not give up
  • Followed the paths of animals
  • Stayed alone in the wilderness
This list may be recorded in the student's notebook.
  Why would following the paths of animals be a possible danger? Why would staying alone in the wilderness be dangerous?

Suggested Student Notes

Courage is being brave—able to face danger without fear.

Cultivating Student Mastery

1. How did Daniel Boone show courage?

The frontier demanded great skill of Daniel Boone.

Student Text, pages 114-115

• Alone in the wilderness, Boone could not depend on anyone but God's Providence to protect and guide him. Boone had developed the skill and dexterity that would be required to escape the Indians.

For Reflection and Reasoning

• What does it mean to have a skill?

• Boone had great skill in the wilderness. He knew the ways of the Indians. How did his skill protect him from Indians?
  How do we know that Boone could make quick decisions? What would have happened if he had seen the Indians, but couldn't decide what he should do?

Cultivating Student Mastery

1. How did Boone show he was a skilful frontiersman?

Patience and steadfastness were required of Daniel Boone

Student Text, pages 115-116

• "This delay, however, was undoubtedly a providential one; for in consequence of the murder of the family of the Indian chief Logan, a terrible Indian war, called in history the Dunmore War, was impending, which broke out in the succeeding year, and extended to that part of the West to which Boone and his party were proceeding..."[55]
  Cecil B. Hartley, *The Life of Daniel Boone*

• Webster defines patience as "The act or quality of waiting long for justice or expected good without discontent."

For Reflection and Reasoning

• What is a settlement?

• Since Daniel Boone could make quick decisions, do you think he liked to wait? Once the decision was made to settle in Kentucky, do you think he would want to move right away? Why couldn't he?

• What is patience? Is it sometimes hard to be patient?

• What does it mean to be steadfast? To be steadfast is to continue with what has been begun. Life for Boone and the pioneers was very difficult. How were Boone and his family steadfast?

Suggested Student Notes

Even with disaster, Boone was steadfast to his dream of a home in Kentucky.

Leading Idea

Boone faced new challenges.

Student Text, pages 116-117

• The following event is not included in the Student Text, but may be included by the Teacher. "Now, biding his time, and longing for greater adventures, Boone receives a message . . . It seems there are certain surveyors who have gone down the Ohio River and have lost themselves in the wilderness. Could Daniel Boone discover these surveyors for the governor? Assuredly. And hence he undertakes his first real mission of independent leadership. He has but one companion, Michael Stoner or Steiner, and before them lie many hundred miles of trackless forest, with no road, no path, no trail. Yet the surveyors are found and led safely back to their own."[56] Another biographer states they traveled "eight hundred miles, through many difficulties, in sixty-two days!"[57]

For Reflection and Reasoning

• What is a leader? When someone is a leader, they may be asked to work harder or longer than those they are leading.

• Daniel Boone was given many opportunities for leadership. Why was he the one that would be asked to purchase land from the Indians? Why had the Indians learned to respect Boone? Would this have helped them trust him?

• Why would Boone be the best man to clear the path of the wilderness trail? Note the picture in the Student Text. What types of tasks were required to clear the wilderness trail? What dangers might have been met while they were clearing the trail? Why would a gun need to be nearby?

• How did Daniel Boone feel about Kentucky?

• Locate Boonesborough on a map.

• What is a palisade? How did the fort and palisade help protect the families of Boonesborough?

Cultivating Student Mastery

1. How did Daniel Boone help many other pioneers get to the frontier?

Cultivating Student Mastery

1. How did the pioneers pay a high price for settling the Western frontier?

Leading Idea

"God gave me a work to perform, and I have done my best."

Student Text, page 118

• ". . . Colonel Boone was visited by the great naturalist, J. J. Audubon, who passed a night with him. In his ornithological Biography, Mr. Audubon gives the following narrative of what passed on that occasion:

"'Daniel Boone . . . happened to spend a night with me under the same roof . . . We had returned from a shooting excursion, in the course of which his extraordinary skill in the management of the rifle had been fully displayed. On retiring to the room appropriated to that remarkable individual and myself for the night, I felt anxious to know more of his exploits and adventures than I did, and accordingly took the liberty of proposing numerous questions to him. The stature and general appearance of this wanderer of the Western forests approached the gigantic. His chest was broad and prominent; his muscular powers displayed themselves in every limb; his countenance gave indication of his great courage, enterprise, and perseverance; and when he spoke, the very motion of his lips brought the impression that whatever he uttered could not be otherwise than strictly true. I undressed, whilst he merely took off his hunting-shirt, and arranged a few folds of blankets on the floor, choosing rather to lie there, as he observed, than on the softest bed. . . .'"[58]

Cecil B. Hartley, *The Life of Daniel Boone*

•"He [Boone] was one of the purest and noblest of the pioneers of the West. Regarding himself as an instrument in the hands of Providence for accomplishing great purposes, he was nevertheless always modest and unassuming, never seeking distinction, but always accepting the post of duty and danger.

"As a military leader he was remarkable for prudence, coolness, bravery, and imperturbable self-possession. His knowledge of the character of the Indians enabled him to divine their intentions and baffle their best laid plans; and notwithstanding his resistance of their inroads, he was always a great favorite amongst them. As a father, husband, and citizen his character seems to have been faultless; and his intercourse with his fellow-men was always marked by the strictest integrity and honor."[59]

Cecil B. Hartley, *The Life of Daniel Boone*

For Reflection and Reasoning

• What character was required of the families that settled in Boonesborough? Were there demands upon these settlers that would not have been present if they had settled in one of the eastern cities? Why?

• What is liberty? Why were the settlers willing to die for their liberty?

• Daniel Boone believed God had given him "a specific work to perform." Use *Student Activity Page 17-3* to conclude the study of Boone. Reasoning from the Student Text, list the contributions of Boone in opening the Western Frontier.

Reflect upon Boone's statement, "God gave me a work to perform, and I have done my best." Does God have a work for each person to perform? Should each person do his best?

Daniel Boone
God's Man for
Opening the Western Frontier

-Loved American liberty
-Encouraged self government in Kentucky
-Was a good example
-Believed God had chosen him to settle the wilderness

"God gave me a work to perform, and I have done my best."

Cultivating Student Mastery

1. Daniel Boone encouraged the settlers to make Kentucky strong. What did he say the settlers would have to do?

2. Why could Daniel Boone be happy at the end of his life?

PIONEER
Westward Movement
Chapters 18-21
6-8 Weeks

Chapter 18
Keeping One Nation under God
3-4 Days

Leading Idea	***Moving West***
	Student Text, page 119

For Reflection and Reasoning

• Who is a Pioneer? America offered the opportunity for families to own land. As the trails were opened — the Wilderness Trail, the Oregon Trail, the California Trail, the Santa Fe Trail, and others — each opened the door to the vast lands of the West. Others followed the Ohio River to reach the Indiana and Wisconsin Territory.

• Locate some of the trails on a map to see the various paths that were taken to go West. Note the geographic difficulties to be faced with each of the trails. *Fur-*

ther study of the pioneer movement will be done in a later year.

• How big was the wagon? What could the Pioneers take with them? Can you imagine putting everything in your house into a wagon, as the pioneers did, and moving thousands of miles west? What would be most important to take with you?

• Discuss the picture in the Student Text. Note how many of the people were walking. Why would many of them have walked? The picture shows horses pulling the wagons. What other animals were sometimes used to pull the wagons?

• What kind of dangers did Daniel Boone face when he went into the wilderness? Would the Pioneers have faced many of the same dangers?

• If you live west of the original thirteen colonies, do you know when your family moved west? Did your great, great grandparents travel in a wagon train? Do you know what route they took?

• What character would it take to face the dangers of moving west as a pioneer.

• See *Student Activity Page 18-1.* Students may color the picture. They may wish to add horses or oxen to pull the wagon and some people and animals walking with the wagon.

Cultivating Student Mastery

1. What character did it take to be a pioneer?

Leading Idea

The liberty in America was built upon self government.

Student Text, page 120.

For Reflection and Reasoning

• Review: What is self government?

• Why would liberty in America require the people to be self governed? What happens if a people are not self governed? Review the charts showing the relationship between self and civil government. See Teacher's Guide, page 26.

• Today, when people come from another country, we call them emigrants. Name some of the countries from which people come that settled in the thirteen colonies. Do you know what country your family was originally from?

• Using the charts relating family government and civil government, consider why it was important for each family to learn to govern themselves? What would happen to civil government if they do not govern themselves?

• What responsibility did each family

have for the new town? How could they be sure that their town would be self governing?

• Use *Student Activity Page 18-2* to review the relationship between a self governing family and a self governing town. Student Notes may be recorded on activity page. The students may draw a picture of their town in the appropriate box.

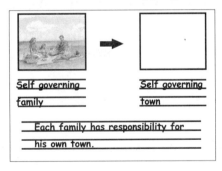

Suggested Student Notes

Each family has responsibility for his own town.

Leading Idea

The obstacles to maintaining a nation of unity with diversity required Biblical character and reasoning.

Student Text, page 120

• When the Declaration of Independence and the Constitution were signed, it was understood that the nation had become one and would stand together. The union of states was built upon the idea that there was unity within the states, yet great diversity. In the Constitution, the national government was given certain responsibility and the balance of civil government was to be with the states, allowing each state to deal with the diversity of that individual state.

• The Scripture teaches that it is the responsibility of each generation to teach the next generation Biblical truth. The United States of America was built upon Biblical principles of government. Those Biblical principles had to be taught to the next generation, in order to maintain the foundation of the nation.

If the Biblical principles were not taught, the people would not continue to have unity.

As the nation grew and prospered, the Biblical unity amongst the states deteriorated. Eventually this produced a division.

• God worked in the hearts of men to keep one nation under God.

For Reflection and Reasoning

• What does it mean to have unity? It means that we are like one. We agree on an idea.

• Do you ever play games at your house? Do you always agree with your brothers and sisters or parents about which game to play? If you do not agree, do you have unity?

• When the Declaration of Independence was signed, did the people in America have unity?

• When the Constitution was approved by the American people, did the people in America have unity?

• On what did they unite? They had to agree on the ideas of how the nation was to be governed. They had to agree on their civil government.

• God gave us our nation. He has given us, in His Word, the ideas on which a nation can be built.

• We must *remember* what God has given us. Review verses on *remembering* what God has done. See Teacher's Guide, page 19.

• When we have liberty to do what we want, it is easy to forget that God has given us that liberty. It is easy to forget the ideas on which our nation was built. By about fifty years after the Constitution, many of the families did not remember all of the ideas of government on which the United States was built. They had lost the unity which had made the United States. In the next chapter, we will see how God prepared someone to lead the United States in this difficult time.

Chapter 19
Abraham Lincoln
10-12 Days

Leading Idea

God prepared Abraham Lincoln to serve America during a very difficult time.

Student Text, page 121.

• "My parents were both born in Virginia, of undistinguished families—second families, perhaps I should say. My mother, who died in my tenth year, was of a family of the name of Hanks, . . . My paternal grandfather, Abraham Lincoln, emigrated from Rockingham County, Virginia, to Kentucky about 1781 or 1782, where a year or two later he was killed by the Indians, not in battle, but by stealth, when he was laboring to open a farm in the forest. His ancestors, who were Quakers, went to Virginia from Berks County, Pennsylvania. . . ."[60]

Abraham Lincoln

• Although not noted in Lincoln's letter, other biographers indicate President Lincoln's grandfather, Abraham Lincoln, was a friend of Daniel Boone's.

For Reflection and Reasoning

• What was the wilderness trail? Daniel Boone led the opening of the wilderness trail in about 1774. How many years later did Abraham Lincoln's grandfather travel along that trail?

• To help the student's relate Washington, Boone, and Abraham Lincoln, prepare a simple timeline identifying key dates. See *Student Activity Page 19-1.* You may note additional dates of importance regarding Washington and Boone.

• How many rooms do you have in your house? Of what are the floors made? How many windows? Note the type of home in which Tom and Nancy Lincoln lived.

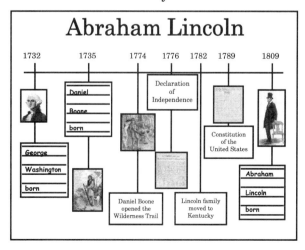

Abraham Lincoln

| 1732 | 1735 | 1774 | 1776 | 1782 | 1789 | 1809 |

Declaration of Independence

Constitution of the United States

Daniel Boone born

George Washington born

Daniel Boone opened the Wilderness Trail

Lincoln family moved to Kentucky

Abraham Lincoln born

"Forsake not the law of thy mother." Proverbs 1:8b.

Student Text, page 122

• Abraham Lincoln's mother died in 1818, at the age of 35 years. There are few written records of Nancy Hanks Lincoln. However, the evidence of her influence upon Abraham Lincoln is great.

• "Abe got his mind and fixed morals

from his good mother. Mrs. Lincoln was a very smart, intelligent, and intellectual woman; she was naturally strong-minded; was a gentle, kind, and tender woman, a Christian of the Baptist persuasion, she was a remarkable woman truly and indeed. . . ."[61]

For Reflection and Reasoning

• Locate Hardin County, Kentucky on a map. Lincoln's birthplace is near the city of Hodgenville, Kentucky.

• Nancy Lincoln was a good mother. What does it mean to be kind and gentle? Using the Student Text, have the students compile a list, identifying Nancy Lincoln's character and contribution to the lives of her children:
  • Kind
  • Gentle
  • Loved God
  • Wanted children to love God
  • Taught children the Bible

• Do you have chores at home? Abe Lin-

coln had many chores. He learned to work hard. Compile a list of Abe Lincoln's chores:
  • Carried water   • Hoed weeds
  • Filled woodbox • Picked berries
  • Ran errands   • Hunted nuts
How many of these chores do you do at your house? *The list could be included as Student Notes, with a title, "Abe learned to work hard."*

Cultivating Student Mastery

1. How did Abe's mother help her family?

2. How did Abe help his family?

3. What character quality did Abe learn by doing chores?

The Lincolns move west to Indiana.

Student Text, page 123

• "He [Abraham Lincoln's father] removed from Kentucky to what is now Spencer County, Indiana, in my eighth year. We reached our new home about the time the State came into the Union. It was a wild region, with many bears and other wild animals still in the woods.

There I grew up. . . . There was absolutely nothing to excite ambition for education. Of course, when I came of age I did not know much. Still, somehow, I could read, write, and cipher to the rule of three, but that was all. I have not been to school since. The little advance I now have upon this store of education, I have picked up from time to time under the pressure of necessity."[62]

Abraham Lincoln

• There is some discrepancy in biographers as to the year of the Lincoln's move to Indiana. Lincoln states it was in his eighth year.

For Reflection and Reasoning

• Locate Little Pigeon Creek, near Lincoln City, Indiana on a map.

• What does it mean to make a claim for a house? If your parents want to have a house, what must they do?

• How did they "clear" the land? What was most unusual about their first house? How did they protect themselves? When they built the new cabin, how did Mother Nancy, Sarah and Abe help?

• Abe Lincoln's mother loved her family very much. She did many things for them. When she died, they were very sad and missed her. Who tried to help with the many tasks at home?

What tasks does your mother have each day at your house? Does she clean, cook, and do laundry? Does she drive you to school or to the library? It would be very difficult if mother could not do those things.

Suggested Student Notes

The American frontier was a land of opportunity for those who would work hard.

Cultivating Student Mastery

1. How could a person earn land, without needing a large sum of money?

2. How did Sarah show courage and love for her family?

Leading Idea

A new mother for Abe and Sarah

Student Text, page 124

• It is difficult to imagine Abe and Sarah being left in the cabin on Little Pigeon Creek for several weeks, while Tom Lincoln traveled back to Kentucky for a new wife. Neighbors were usually some miles away. It would seem that Sarah and Abe were able to take great responsibility at a very young age.

For Reflection and Reasoning

• How did Mr. Lincoln travel back to Kentucky? When he returned with his new wife, what types of things did they bring with them?

• Describe the bed on which you sleep. Can you imagine what a bed made of corn husks would be like? Were feather pillows and a feather mattress better than a bed of corn husks? Have you ever seen a feather mattress? How are they different from the beds of today? Do you think Abe and Sarah enjoyed the new furniture and things at their house?

• The new mother loved Abe and Sarah. What would it mean to have "a mother's care back in the home"?

Cultivating Student Mastery

1. How did the new mother help the Lincoln family?

Abe Lincoln loved to read and learn.

Student Text, page 125

• Although Lincoln had limited formal education, he demonstrated an eagerness for learning and the success of self education. It appears that he took every opportunity to read and study.

• Late in her life, Sarah Bush Lincoln, the stepmother to Abraham, wrote her recollections of Abraham: "Abe slept upstairs, went up on pins stuck in the logs, like a ladder; our bedsteads were original creations, none such now, made of poles and clapboards. Abe was about nine years of age when I landed in Indiana. The country was wild and desolate. Abe was a good boy; he didn't like physical labor, was diligent for knowledge, wished to know, and if pains and labor would get it, he was sure to get it. He was the best boy I ever saw. He read all the books he could lay his hands on. . . . Abe read the Bible some. . . I think newspapers were had in Indiana as early as 1824 . . . Abe was a constant reader of them. . . Abe read history papers and other books . . . He duly reverenced old age, loved those best about his own age, played with those under his age; he listened to the aged, argued with his equals, but played with the children. He loved animals generally and treated them kindly; he loved children well, very well. . . . Abe didn't care much for crowds of people; he chose his own company, which was always good. . . . When Abe was reading, my husband took particular care not to disturb him, would let him read on and on till Abe quit of his own accord. He was dutiful to me always; he loved me truly, I think."[63]

For Reflection and Reasoning

• How much was Abe Lincoln able to go to school? Yet, how do we know he learned to read well? What books did he especially like to read? Of all the books Abe Lincoln read, which ones have you read?

• Whose responsibility is it to learn? How much did Abe Lincoln love learning?

Cultivating Student Mastery

1. How much did Abe Lincoln love learning? How do you know?

2. How did Lincoln show respect for property that belonged to someone else?

Abe loved life but worked hard.

Student Text, pages 125-126

• Lincoln described himself — "If any personal description of me is thought desirable, it may be said I am, in height, six feet four inches, nearly; lean in flesh, weighing on an average one hundred and eighty pounds; dark complexion, with coarse black hair and grey eyes. No other marks or brands recollected."[64]

● Lincoln was described by his law partner, William H. Herndon — "It is now the time to describe the person of Mr. Lincoln: he was about six feet four inches high, . . . He was thin, wiry, sinewy, raw and big heavy-boned, thin through the breast to the back and narrow across the shoulders, standing he leaned forward; was what may be called stoop-shouldered, inclining to the consumptively built, his usual weight being about one hundred and sixty or eighty pounds. . . . . The whole man, body and mind, worked slowly, creakingly, as if it needed oiling. Physically he was a very powerful man, lifting, as said, with ease four or six hundred pounds. . . . When this man moved and walked along he moved and walked cautiously, but firmly, his long and big bony arms and hands on them, hanging like giant hands on them, swung by his side; he walked with even tread, . . . The very first opinion that a stranger or one who did not observe closely would form of Lincoln's walk and motion was that he was a tricky man, a man of cunning, a dangerous shrewd man, one to watch closely and not to be trusted, but his walk was the manifested walk of caution and firmness. . . . His legs and arms were, as compared with the average man, abnormally, unnaturally long, though when compared to his own organism, the whole physical man, these organs may have been in harmony with the man. His arms and hands, feet and legs, seemed to me, as compared with the average man, in undue proportion to the balance of his body. It was only when Lincoln rose on his feet that he loomed up above the mass of men. He looked the giant then. . . .

"Thus I say stood, walked, looked, felt, thought, willed, and acted this peculiar and singular man; he was odd, angular, homely, but when those little gray eyes and face were lighted up by the inward soul on fires of emotion, defending the liberty of man or proclaiming the truths of the Declaration of Independence, or defending justice and the eternal right, then it was that all those apparently ugly or homely features sprang into organs of beauty, or sank themselves into the sea of his inspiration that on such occasions flooded up his many face. Sometimes it did appear to me that Lincoln was just fresh from the presence and hands of his Creator."[65]

For Reflection and Reasoning

● How do you know that Abe Lincoln enjoyed fun?

● How do you know he obeyed his stepmother?

● What does it mean to split logs? Why did they split logs? What did they do with the logs?

● Lincoln loved learning and reading, but didn't really enjoy the farm work. Yet, how did he do the farm work? Was he diligent, even in the work he did not enjoy?

Cultivating Student Mastery

1. Ecclesiastes 9:10 says, "Whatsoever thy hand findeth to do, do it with all thy might . . . " How did Abe Lincoln live up to this verse?

Leading Idea

Moving further west

Student Text, pages 126-127

● As frontier lands became more populated, many pioneers would move further west. They were always looking for new lands and plenty of room.

For Reflection and Reasoning

• Locate Indiana, Illinois and the Wabash River on the map. The Lincoln family crossed the Wabash River near Vincennes, Indiana.

• Read poem:

> ### All Things Bright and Beautiful
> Cecil Frances Alexander
>
> All things bright and beautiful,
> All creatures great and small,
> All things wise and wonderful,
> The Lord God made them all.

• How did Lincoln show that he cared for all of God's creatures?

• Did reading the Bible and Aesop's fables teach Lincoln to love all of God's creatures?

• Lincoln was known for his great physical strength. It is said he could split rails better than any other. Does splitting four hundred rails seem like a lot of work for each yard of cloth?

• When you go to visit your grandparents or take a vacation, do you pack a suitcase? How large is it? How large was the package which Lincoln took when he left to make his own living?

• See *Student Activity Page 19-2*. Reason with the students concerning Abe Lincoln's actions to determine what character quality was demonstrated.

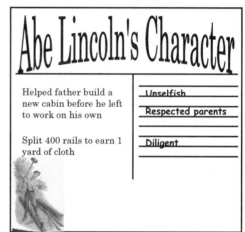

Abe Lincoln's Character

| Helped father build a new cabin before he left to work on his own | Unselfish |
| Respected parents |
| Split 400 rails to earn 1 yard of cloth | Diligent |

Leading Idea

Honesty is the best policy.

Student Text, pages 127– 128

For Reflection and Reasoning

• What is a clerk? How did Lincoln spend his free time when there were no customers in the store? How does this show his love of learning?

• What does it mean to be honest? Why was Abe Lincoln called "Honest Abe"?

• What is a postmaster? Describe the unusual manner in which Lincoln delivered letters. How are letters delivered to your house?

• Abe Lincoln was not known for his good looks. What did people often remember about him?

Cultivating Student Mastery

• Which is more important, good looks or good character? Why?

Lincoln was successful in public life.

Student Text, pages 129-130

• "I was raised to farm work, which I continued till I was twenty-two. At twenty-two I came to Illinois, Macon County. Then I got to New Salem, at that time in Sangamon, now in Menard County, where I remained a year as a sort of clerk in a store. Then came the Black Hawk war; and I was elected a captain of volunteers, a success which gave me more pleasure than any I have had since. I went the campaign, was elated, ran for the legislature the same year (1832), and was beaten—the only time I ever have been beaten by the people. The next and three succeeding biennial elections I was elected to the legislature. I was not a candidate afterward. During this legislative period I had studied law, and removed to Springfield to practise it. In 1846 I was once elected to the lower House of Congress. Was not a candidate for reelection. From 1849 to 1854, both inclusive, practised law more assiduously than ever before. Always a Whig in politics: and generally on the Whig electoral tickets, making active canvasses. I was losing interest in politics when the repeal of the Missouri compromise aroused me again. What I have done since then is pretty well known."[66]

Abraham Lincoln

For Reflection and Reasoning

• Review: What is law? How are laws made?

• Lincoln's first public office was to the Illinois legislature. Where did the legislature meet? What does the legislature do?

• How does someone become a lawyer today? How did Lincoln become a lawyer?

• When Lincoln worked in the store, he was known for always being honest. Reason with the students to compile a list illustrating how Abraham Lincoln practiced honesty when he became a lawyer.
  • Only represented just claims
  • Never charged extra
  • Took no money from the poor
This list, or selected points, could be recorded as Student Notes.

• Why did people want Abe Lincoln to be their representative?

• How did Lincoln's time as a clerk prepare him to be a lawyer and a representative?

All men are created equal.

Student Text, page 130

• Lincoln reasoned from the Declaration of Independence, following the Dred Scott Decision by the Supreme Court. "I think the authors of that notable instrument intended to include *all* men, but they did not intend to declare all men equal *in all respects.* They did not mean to say all were equal in color, size, intellect, moral developments, or social capacity. They defined with tolerable distinctness in what respects they did consider all men created equal—equal with 'certain inalienable rights, among which are life, liberty, and the pursuit of happiness.' This they said, and this they meant. They did not mean to assert the obvious untruth that all were then actually enjoying that equality, nor yet that they were about to confer it immediately upon them. In fact, they had no power to confer such a boon. They meant simply to declare the right, so that enforcement of it might follow as fast as circumstances should permit.

"They meant to set up a standard maxim for free society, which should be familiar to all, and revered by all; constantly looked to, constantly labored for, and even though never perfectly at-tained, constantly approximated, and thereby constantly spreading and deepening its influence and augmenting the happiness and value of life to all people of all colors everywhere. The assertion that 'all men are created equal' was of no practical use in effecting our separation from Great Britain; and it was placed in the Declaration not for that, but for future use. Its authors meant it to be—as, thank God, it is now proving itself—a stumbling block to all those who in after times might seek to turn a free people back into the hateful paths of despotism. They knew the proneness of prosperity to breed tyrants, and they meant when such should reappear in this fair land and commence their vocation, they should find left for them at least one hard nut to crack."[67]

Abraham Lincoln

For Reflection and Reasoning

• Review: Who is the President? Who was the first President?

• Throughout history, there have been people who have been held by others as slaves. Note the time of Moses in Egypt. The Children of Israel were slaves under Pharaoh. What is a slave?

• As the American states began, some individuals bought slaves and used them to help with their work, particularly on the southern plantations.

• The Word of God teaches that each per-son is important and has value. The Declaration of Independence said that "all men were created equal." Lincoln knew that slavery was wrong.

• As new states were being brought into the United States, Lincoln did not want the new states to allow slavery. He made speeches to try to reason with the people.

• When Lincoln became President, the nation was facing a great problem. What was the problem?

Cultivating Student Mastery

1. Why is slavery wrong?

Leading Idea

"A house divided against itself cannot stand."

Student Text, pages 130-131

• Lincoln delivered the following address at the Republican State Convention in Illinois, June 16, 1858. *"Mr. President and* *Gentlemen of the Convention:* If we could first know where we are, and whither we are tending, we could better judge what to do, and how to do it. We are now far into the fifth year since a policy was initiated with the avowed object and confident promise of putting an end to slavery agitation. Under the operation of that policy, that agitation has not only not ceased, but has constantly augmented. In my opinion, it will not cease until a crisis shall have been reached and passed. 'A house divided against itself cannot stand.' I believe this government cannot endure permanently half slave and half free. I do not expect the Union to be dissolved—I do not expect the house to fall—but I do expect it will cease to be divided. It will become all one thing, or all the other. Either the opponents of slavery will arrest the further spread of it, and place it where the public mind shall rest in the belief that it is in the course of ultimate extinction; or its advocates will push it forward till it shall become alike lawful in all the States, old as well as new, North as well as South."[68]

• "I would save the Union. I would save it the shortest way under the Constitution. The sooner the national authority can be restored, the nearer the Union will be 'the Union as it was.' If there be those who would not save the Union unless they could at the same time save slavery, I do not agree with them. If there be those who would not save the Union unless they could at the same time destroy slavery, I do not agree with them. My paramount object in this struggle is to save the Union, and is not either to save or to destroy slavery. If I could save the Union without freeing any slave, I would do it; and if I could save it by freeing all the slaves, I would do it; and if I could save it by freeing some and leaving others alone, I would also do that. What I do about slavery and the colored race I do because I believe it helps to save the Union; and what I forebear, I forebear because I do not believe it would help to save the Union. "[69]

For Reflection and Reasoning

• Read Matthew 12:25. Consider the phrase: "A house divided against itself cannot stand." How would a house be divided against itself? When Lincoln was speaking about America, what did he mean? How would America be divided against itself?

• Review: How do you have unity between two or more people?

• The American people did not agree about slavery, but even more important, the American people were divided about whether they must stay together as one nation. The Southern states had withdrawn from the United States and formed a new civil government. The question was union, not slavery.

• The war that began between the North and the South was a very sad war. What made it so sad?

• What was Lincoln's main concern?

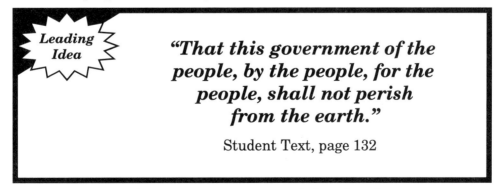

★ **Leading Idea**

"That this government of the people, by the people, for the people, shall not perish from the earth."

Student Text, page 132

• *"My dear Sir:* You ask me to put in writing the substance of what I verbally said the other day in your presence, . . . 'I am naturally antislavery. If slavery is not wrong, nothing is wrong. I cannot remember when I did not so think and feel, and yet I have never understood that the presidency conferred upon me an unrestricted right to act officially upon this judgment and feeling. It was in the oath I took that I would, to the best of my ability, preserve, protect, and defend the Constitution of the United States. . . . I did understand, however, that my oath to preserve the Constitution to the best of my ability imposed upon me the duty of preserving, by every indispensable means, that government—that nation, of which that Constitution was the organic law. Was it possible to lose the nation and yet preserve the Constitution? . . . I could not feel that, to the best of my ability, I had even tried to preserve the Constitution, if, to save slavery or any minor matter, I should permit the wreck of government, country, and Constitution all together. . . .

"Now, at the end of three years' struggle, the nation's condition is not what either party, or any man, devised or expected. God alone can claim it. Whither it is tending seems plain. If God now wills the removal of a great wrong, and wills also that we of the North, as well as you of the South, shall pay fairly for our complicity in that wrong, impartial history will find therein new cause to attest and revere the just and goodness of God."[70]

• "The Almighty has his own purposes. 'Woe unto the world because of offenses!

For it must needs be that offenses come; but woe to that man by whom the offense cometh.' If we shall suppose that American slavery is one of those offenses which, in the providence of God, must needs come, but which, having continued through his appointed time, he now wills to remove, and that he gives to both North and South this terrible war, as the woe due to those by whom the offense came, shall we discern therein any departure from those divine attributes which the believers in a living God always ascribe to him? Fondly do we hope—fervently do we pray—that this mighty scourge of war may speedily pass away. Yet, if God wills that it continue until all the wealth piled by the bondman's two hundred and fifty years of unrequited toil shall be sunk, and until every drop of blood drawn with the lash shall be paid by another drawn with the sword, as was said three thousand years ago, so still it must be said, 'The judgments of the Lord are true and righteous altogether.'

"With malice toward none; with charity for all; with firmness in the right, as God gives us to see the right, let us strive on to finish the work we are in; to bind up the nation's wounds; to care for him who shall have borne the battle, and for his widow, and his orphan—to do all which may achieve and cherish a just and lasting peace among ourselves, and with all nations."[71]

Abraham Lincoln,
Second Inaugural Address

For Reflection and Reasoning

• Review: What is government? What is civil government?

• Review: What is Providence?

• How would government be "of the people"? How would it be "by the people"? What is the purpose of civil government? How would it be "for the people"?

• Read Esther 4:14b. How was Abraham Lincoln the President God used for "just such a time as this?"

• How does Abraham Lincoln's life remind us that God uses the small as well as the great to accomplish His plan?

• Guide the students to prepare a sentence identifying Abraham Lincoln's contribution to the nation. Students may record as Student Notes.

Chapter 20
Communication across a Nation
10-15 Days

• Noah Webster defined *communicate* as "To impart; to give to another. . . To confer for joint possession." He defined *communication* as "Interchange of thoughts or opinions. . . Interchange of knowledge; . . . Good understanding between men."

• From 1620 to 1776, the Colonists communicated and refined their ideas concerning self and civil government. These ideas were communicated through letters, pamphlets and books.

The colonists had come to the New World from many different nations. They had grown up with different views of church and civil government.

In America, as the Biblical ideas of self and civil government were preached and declared in writing, these ideas brought a unity of understanding.

"The colonies had grown up under constitutions of government so different, there was so great a variety of religions, they were composed of so many different nations, their customs, manners and habits had so little resemblance, and their intercourse had been so rare, and their knowledge of each other so imperfect, that to unite them in the same principles in theory, and the same system of action, was certainly a very difficult enterprise. The complete accomplishment of it, in so short a time and by such simple means, was, perhaps, a singular example in the history of mankind— Thirteen clocks were made to strike together; a perfection of mechanism which no artist had ever before effected."[72]

For Reflection and Reasoning

• Define communication. Perhaps an appropriate student definition would be "Exchanging thoughts or ideas with another." What does it mean to exchange thoughts? How do we exchange thoughts? Students may record the definition in their notebook.

• If you want someone in your family, or a friend, to understand something that you are thinking, how do you help them to understand? Would you tell them what you are thinking?

• If you want a person to understand an idea, but the person is not where you are, how can you tell them your idea?

• If you are going to play a game, do each of the players need to understand how to play and agree on the rules?

• The early American colonists considered what the Bible taught about self government and about the nation. They each wanted the people in the other colonies to understand the same ideas. They wrote letters, printed pamphlets or books, and sent them to others.

Cultivating Student Mastery

1. What is communication?

2. In what ways do we communicate with others?

Leading Idea

Common language aids in bringing unity to a nation

Student Text, pages 134-135

• Noah Webster defined a nation as "A body of people inhabiting the same country, or united under the same sovereign or government. . . The word *nation* usually denotes a body of people speaking the same language."

• Many of America's colonists came from England, but some came from non-English speaking countries. The colonists recognized that they must have one language to communicate and unite together in purpose as a nation.

After the nation was formed, immigrants came from many nations. They came to America to enjoy freedom. They wanted freedom to worship God according to their conscience. They were looking for the freedom to own property.

And when they came, they were no longer French, German, Italian, Chinese, Spanish, African, or English. They knew they were Americans.

• God used Noah Webster to unify the American English. His dictionary identified new definitions as Americans refined their understanding of government. His *Blue-backed Speller* unified the language in spelling.

• "Said Southerner Jefferson Davis: 'We have a unity of language no other people possess, and we owe this unity, above all else, to Noah Webster's Yankee Spelling-Book.'"[73]

For Reflection and Reasoning

• Review: What is communication? Why is it important to communicate?

• If you moved to France, what language would you need to learn to communicate with the people in France? If you moved to Spain, what language would you need to learn to communicate?

As people came to America, they knew they must learn the language of **this** nation.

• Demonstrate for the students the need for a common language. 1. Speak to the students in a foreign language to see if they can understand. 2. Write a sentence on the board in another language and also in English. 3. Show the students a book in another language to see if they can read it.

Help the students recognize how difficult communication would be if people in a nation could not speak or read the same language.

• Have you met someone who does not speak English? How do you communicate with them? If we want to agree, would we need to understand one another?

• Why is it important for the people in one nation to speak one language?

• Noah Webster wrote many books — *The Blue-backed Speller* helped all Americans to learn to spell words the same way. This helped bring unity to the nation.

• Noah Webster also wrote another extremely important book, *The American Dictionary of the English Language*. What is a dictionary? What does a dictionary help us learn or understand? Several times this year we have looked at definitions that Noah Webster wrote in his *Dictionary*.

The people in America learned about governing themselves from the Bible. But many words about government meant something different in this nation than in England or the other nations from which the colonists came. Noah Webster defined those words in his *Dictionary*. He wrote the definitions according to the way the words were used in the King James Bible.

• If a copy of the 1828 *Dictionary* is available, let the students see the work which Noah Webster spent so many years preparing. Look at a selected word to see how he identified the language from which the word came. Students would also enjoy seeing Webster's picture in the front of the *Dictionary*.

• Noah Webster finished the *Dictionary* in 1828. He taught himself 26 languages to complete the *Dictionary*. He wanted to be able to show the language from which each word came. It took him 28 years to complete his work.

He wrote many other textbooks, a history book, and translated the Bible from the original languages of Greek and Hebrew.

The students will study more about Noah Webster in another year.

• The students might enjoy looking up a word in the *Dictionary*.

• *Student Activity Page 20-1.* Students read quote from Jefferson Davis and color the picture of Noah Webster.

Cultivating Student Mastery

1. Which two of Noah Webster's books helped to unite the language of Americans?

2. Why was it important to develop new ways to communicate in America?

Leading Idea

Talents and ideas are internal property.

• "Property . . . In the former sense, a man's land, or merchandise, or money, is called his property. In the latter sense, a man has a property in his opinions and the free communication of them. He has a property of peculiar value in his religious opinions, and in the profession, and practice dictated by them . . . In a word, as a man is said to have a right to his property, he may be equally said to have a property in his rights."[74]

For Reflection and Reasoning

• Review the ideas concerning owning personal property as discussed in the study of the Pilgrims.

• Develop a simple chart identifying internal and external property. Suggestions have been included, but the teacher may personalize the chart to reflect the student's individuality and interest. This chart could be recorded in the student notebook.

• Consider the two spheres of property: internal and external. When we think about property, we usually think about things that we own, such as our toys, bicycles, books, and clothes. We may think about property that our family owns, such as furniture, dishes, a car, or our house.

God has also given us property that is internal. What kind of property do we have that is internal? Do you have ideas? Can you play the piano or another musical instrument? Do you like to draw? These are called talents. How do you have those talents? Did God give them to you?

Internal Property	External Property
Ideas	Books
Thoughts	Clothes
Talents	Toys
Feelings	Bicycle
Temper	Notebook

Leading Idea

God prepares individuals for His purpose — Samuel F. B. Morse

Student Text, pages 135-137

• As the need for communication grew in America, God provided the individual who would answer the need. That man was Samuel Morse and the answer was the telegraph.

• Samuel Morse pursued his God-given talent for painting, while simultaneously continuing his inquiries into the field of electricity.

For Reflection and Reasoning

• Samuel Morse went to Europe to further his study and mastery of painting. But God used this trip for another purpose. What new things did Samuel learn on the trip to Europe? What ideas did God give him? What did he do with those ideas?

• Reason from the Student Text concerning God's Hand in setting the right stage for Morse to develop the idea of the telegraph. How did God prepare Morse at the right time for this invention?

• Show the students a picture of a telegraph. You may wish to expand the ideas presented in the text concerning the mechanics of a telegraph.

• Reason from the Student Text concerning the unique talents which God had given Samuel F. B. Morse. The teacher may help the students compose a sentence identifying the gift(s) which God had given to Samuel Morse. The sentence may be recorded as Student Notes.

Cultivating Student Mastery

1. How did God prepare Samuel Morse to invent the telegraph?

Leading Idea

"America's Heritage of Christian Character" — diligence and industry

Student Text, pages 137-140

• Webster defines *diligence* as "Steady application in business of any kind; constant effort to accomplish what is undertaken," and *industry* as "Habitual diligence."

• As a child, Samuel Morse found it difficult to concentrate on any task for very long. He was quickly drawn away to *new* interests. This character had to be changed, since the development of the telegraph took many years of research and testing.

• In order to lay telegraph wires, Morse appealed to Congress for the necessary funds. Again and again, he was turned away. Finally in March, 1843, Congress voted to lay the first telegraph lines.

For Reflection and Reasoning

• Review: 1) The definition of character. See Teacher's Guide, page 110. 2) The idea that *character is produced through difficulties.*

• What does it mean to be diligent? Was

Samuel Morse diligent as a boy?

• Have students record a simple definition of diligence.

• Samuel Morse faced many difficulties. How did these difficulties help him develop the character of diligence?

• *Student Activity Page 20-2.* Reasoning from the Student Text, identify the difficulties which Samuel Morse faced in

developing the telegraph. Opposite from the difficulties, record how Samuel Morse demonstrated diligence in overcoming difficulties.

• Why would the people in a self governing nation need to be diligent?

Suggested Student Notes

Diligence is steady work at any task.

 **Leading Idea**

"What hath God wrought"

Student Text, pages 140-141

• Samuel Morse wrote to his brother Sidney on May 31, 1844:
"Dear Sidney,

"You will see by the papers, how great success has attended the first efforts of the Telegraph. That sentence of Annie Ellsworth's was divinely indited, for it is in my thoughts day and night. 'What hath God wrought.' It is his work, and he alone could have carried me thus far through all my trials, and enabled me to triumph over the obstacles physical and moral which opposed me. 'Not unto us, not unto us, but to thy name O Lord be all the praise.' — I begin to fear now the effects of public favor, lest it should kindle that pride of heart and self sufficiency, which dwells in my own, as well as in other's breasts, and which alas! Is so ready to be inflamed by the slightest spark of praise. I do indeed feel gratified, and it is right I should rejoice, but I rejoice with fear, and I desire that a sense of dependence upon, and increased obligation to the Giver of every good and perfect gift, may keep me humble, and circumspect.

"The Convention at Baltimore happened most opportunely for the display of the powers of the Telegraph, especially as it was the medium of correspondence in one instance between the De-

mocratic Convention and the first candidate elect for the Vice Presidency. The enthusiasm of the crowd before the window of the Telegraph Room in the Capitol, was excited to the highest pitch, at the announcement of the nomination of the Presidential Candidate, and the whole of it afterwards Seemer turned upon the Telegraph. They gave the Telegraph 3 cheers, and I was called to make my appearance at the window, when three cheers were given to me by some hundreds present, composed mainly of members of Congress. Such is the feeling in Congress that many tell me, they are ready to grant any thing. Even the most inveterate opposers, have changed to admirers and one of them Hon. Cave Johnson, who ridiculed my system last session by associating it with the tricks of animal magnetism, came to me and said, 'Sir I give in, it is an astonishing invention.' When I see all this, and such enthusiasm everywhere manifested, and contrast the present with the past season of darkness and almost despair, have I not occasion to exclaim 'What hath God wrought'? Surely none but He who has all hearts in his hands, and turns them as the rivers of waters are turned, could so have brought light out of darkness. Sorrow may continue for a night but joy cometh in the morning. Pray for me then, my dear brother, that I may have a heart to praise the Great Deliverer, and in future when discour-aged or despairing be enabled to remember His past mercy and in full faith rest all my cares on him who careth for us. . ."[75]

For Reflection and Reasoning

• Inventors find new ways to do things. Who gives the inventors their ideas? How does Samuel Morse's letter show that he knew God had given him the idea for the telegraph?

• Reason with the students from Samuel Morse's letter, Student Text page 140, to write a statement regarding his dependence upon God. Record this conclusion as Student's Notes.

• Introduce the students to the Morse Code. See Teacher's Guide, page 172. The students would enjoy writing a short sentence, or perhaps their name, using Morse Code. If possible, allow the students to "hear" the Morse Code, using a tape, or via the internet.

Leading Idea

God prepares individuals for His purpose — Alexander Graham Bell

Student Text, pages 141-144

• In God's wisdom, He placed Bell in a home which would focus Alexander's attention on hearing and speech. His mother was nearly deaf and his father had developed a special system for forming sounds and words which he called *visible speech*. Bell was also given unusual talent in the field of music, further developing his gift for hearing sounds. This played a major role in his work with the deaf, and, eventually, his work on the telephone.

Many of Bell's early experiments involved the use of tuning forks. Bell was extremely sensitive to the slightest variations in sound.

For Reflection and Reasoning

• Reason from the Student Text to identify the special characteristics of Alexander Graham Bell's home which prepared him for his work with the deaf and for the invention of the telephone.

• God gives each individual the talents to fulfill His purpose. What unique talent did God give to Alexander which would assist in his future work?

Cultivating Student Mastery

1. What unique talent did God give Alexander Graham Bell which assisted in his future work?

Leading Idea

Sound from afar

Student Text, pages 144-146

• The word *telephone* comes from two Greek words: *tele*, which means far off and *phone,* which means sound.

• Bell was convinced that he could find a way to transmit the human voice over wire. While endeavoring to improve upon the telegraph, his idea was confirmed. Bell and Watson were experimenting with organ reeds. Working in separate rooms, they made the reed vibrate on a transmitter. The sound of the vibration would be received in another room.

One day, one of the organ reeds on Watson's side did not work properly. He had adjusted a screw too tightly. He tried to make the reed work by flicking it with his fingers. With his sensitive, musical ear, Bell immediately heard the different sound. He heard variation in the sound. This was the breakthrough that Bell needed. He now knew it would be possible to transmit speech, with its change in pitch and volume, over a wire.

For Reflection and Reasoning

• Can you imagine living today without a telephone? How do you and your family use the telephone? We call our friends and make plans to get together. Mom and Dad take care of things for the family. If you have to go to the doctor, Mom or Dad calls the doctor's office to set up an appointment. Many people even carry a telephone with them. The telephone is a helpful tool for communication

• Many of Bell's earliest experiments involved music. He realized that sound was carried in the air. Certain sounds could even make another object vibrate.

The students might enjoy experimenting with forks. Tap the fork on a table, then put the fork to your ear and listen to the sound. Different forks will produce different pitches.

• Reason with the students concerning the character required for Bell to develop his idea of the telephone.

• It is always easier to experiment with what another has discovered. Many inventions have been built upon the ideas developed by Alexander Graham Bell. God has used individuals throughout history to open the path for others to follow. It may be the discovery of a New World, or a new invention. Once the way has been shown, it is easy for others to follow that path.

• The students might enjoy making their own telephone. Materials needed: 2 paper cups, 2 paper clips, scissors, and string.
1. Poke a hole in the bottoms of the two cups.
2. Cut a piece of string about 25 feet long.
3. Pull one end of the string through the bottom of one cup.
4. Fasten a paper clip to the string inside the cup. Tie a knot. This will keep the string in place.

5. Repeat steps 3 and 4 with the other paper cup and the other end of the string.
6. Each person holds a cup. Walk away from each other so the string is taut.
7. One person holds cup to his or her ear while the other person talks into cup at the opposite end of the string.
8. Observe the sound that is transmitted from one cup to the other.

When one person speaks into the cup, the bottom of that cup vibrates. The bottom of the cup is like a diaphragm. These vibrations travel along the string and through the bottom of the other cup. The bottom of this cup is also like a diaphragm. The sound waves are then heard by the listener. The result is sound.

Variations: Substitute plastic cups, tin cans, or oatmeal boxes for the paper cups. Substitute wire, ribbon, or rope for the string. Observe which materials transmit the best sounds.[76]

Ideas from *Alexander Graham Bell*
Patricia Ryon Quiri

Leading Idea

Communication from coast to coast

Student Text, pages 146-148

• Bell had no idea that the telephone would be used as extensively as it is today. It is said that he told people the telephone was for calling out, not for calling in.

• Bell faced many challenges regarding the invention of the telephone. These resulted in many patent suits. In a letter to his wife, he wrote — "Oh! Mabel dear—please please PLEASE (that's copied from you) make me write. Make me describe and publish my ideas that I may at least obtain credit for them and that people may know that I am still alive and working and thinking. I can't bear to hear that even my friends should think that I stumbled upon an invention and there is no more good in me."[77]

• Alexander Graham Bell worked in many fields of discovery. One early effort was later developed into communications via laser. He improved the recorder for Edison's phonograph, and, with others, solved the problem of stability of balance in a flying machine.

For Reflection and Reasoning

• Have you ever talked with someone, using a telephone, who lives in another state? Could you call someone in another country? In 1915, Alexander Graham Bell made the first call from New York to California.

• How could using the telephone help people in a nation to stay united? Or, how could it help them to separate?

• See *Student Activity Page 20-3.* Starting with Bell's original telephone, follow the wire to review the development of the telephone.

● Alexander Graham Bell worked on many other inventions beside the telephone. Some of his work was used later by others to develop new inventions for communication. He also improved inventions others had made.

● Use *Student Activity Pages 20-4* and *20-5,* to review the history of communication across the nation. Using the Student Text, complete the dates on the timeline,then cut and glue pictures as indicated.

Cultivating Student Mastery

1. How did communication help to unite the nation?

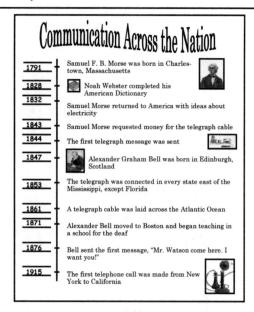

Communication Across the Nation

1791	Samuel F. B. Morse was born in Charlestown, Massachusetts
1828	Noah Webster completed his American Dictionary
1832	Samuel Morse returned to America with ideas about electricity
1843	Samuel Morse requested money for the telegraph cable
1844	The first telegraph message was sent
1847	Alexander Graham Bell was born in Edinburgh, Scotland
1853	The telegraph was connected in every state east of the Mississippi, except Florida
1861	A telegraph cable was laid across the Atlantic Ocean
1871	Alexander Bell moved to Boston and began teaching in a school for the deaf
1876	Bell sent the first message, "Mr. Watson come here. I want you!"
1915	The first telephone call was made from New York to California

Morse Code

A	.-	N	-.	0	-----
B	-...	O	---	1	.----
C	-.-.	P	.--.	2	..---
D	-..	Q	--.-	3	...--
E	.	R	.-.	4	....-
F	..-.	S	...	5	.....
G	--.	T	-	6	-....
H	....	U	..-	7	--...
I	..	V	...-	8	---..
J	.---	W	.--	9	----.
K	-.-	X	-..-		
L	.-..	Y	-.--		
M	--	Z	--..		

Ä	.-.-	Full-stop (period)	.-.-.-
Á	.--.-	Comma	--..--
Å	.--.-	Colon	---...
Ch	----	Quest. mark (query)	..--..
É	..-..	Apostrophe	.----.
Ñ	--.--	Hyphen	-....-
Ö	---.	Fraction bar	-..-.
Ü	..--	Brackets (parenth.)	-.--.-
		Quotation marks	.-..-.

Chapter 21
The Nation Expands
5-7 Days

Leading Idea	One Nation under God — The United States of America
	Student Text, page 149

• One Nation under God — this phrase reflects the foundation of the nation being built upon Biblical principles of government. The unity of the nation comes through uniting upon Biblical principles.

• As new states joined the union, they, too, were expected to embrace the Biblical principles of government. Each state must be One State under God, uniting to be One Nation under God.

For Reflection and Reasoning

• Review: What document was written in Philadelphia in 1787? Who wrote the document?

• Each of the thirteen states had to approve the Constitution. By what year was that completed? Who became the first President?

• Note the picture in the Student Text. How many stars are on the flag? What did each star represent?

• How many states are now in the United States? Look at the map of the United States on page 152 of the Student Text. Locate the thirteen original colonies. Locate the state in which you live. What are the names of the states which surround your state? Locate Hawaii, the

last state to become part of the United States. Look at a globe or larger map to find the location of Alaska and Hawaii.

• How many states have been added to the United States since the Constitution was approved in 1789?

• Prepare a flag of the original thirteen states, using colored paper. Use red paper as the background. Glue on six appropriately spaced white stripes. Glue on a blue rectangle in the top left corner. Glue on thirteen stars or affix star stickers,
   Note: This activity would probably consume one class time.

• Sing familiar patriotic songs. Examples: *Hats Off!; The Star Spangled Banner; My Country 'Tis of Thee; America the Beautiful.*

 **Leading Idea**

The nation expanded.

Student Text, page 150

• As the Republic expanded, it was anticipated that each state was prepared for local self government. This demanded, first, that the individual families were practicing self government.

"To put the power in the people implies faith. It implies that the component individuals are, for the most part, already endowed with self-control. This Republic is grounded in the belief that the individual can govern himself. On the validity of that belief it will stand—or fall."[78]

Felix Morley, *The Power in the People*

For Reflection and Reasoning

• Note the picture in the Student Text. How many stars are on the flag? What does each star represent?

• Review: What is self government? How does each state govern themselves?

• How is the method of a state becoming part of the United States of America built upon the idea of self government?

• The Constitution included a plan for new states to join the United States. Did the founding fathers think there would be additional states?

• Begin to compile a list of the steps which are taken for a state to be part of the United States.
  • The people of the territory must choose to be part of the United States.
  • Representatives write a state constitution.
  • People agree to the state constitution.

• Color a picture of the United States flag. Note the arrangement of the stars. How many stars are in each row? Note the alternating rows.

 **Leading Idea**

New states must protect the ideas of liberty and self government.

Student Text, page 151

• Continue compiling a list of the steps for a state to be part of the United States.
  • Congress must approve the new state.

• Review: What is a representative?

• Who is the Congress of the United States? Where does the Congress meet?

What is the job of the Congress?

• See *Student Activity Page 21-1.* What ideas must be part of the state constitution?

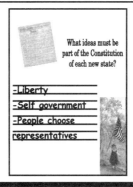

• The history of each state is unique. In a later year, time will be dedicated to the history of the state. The current year's study provides the opportunity to identify basic information concerning the state in which the student lives. You may wish to contact your senator or representative for information.

If time allows, this study could be expanded to include other states of interest.

Leading Idea

Each State has its own history.

• See *Student Activity Page 21-2.* Using a simple children's encyclopedia or simple book about the state, students may research their individual state.

When did your state become a part of the United States? Where does your state rank in the 50 states, i.e. Indiana is the 19th state, Hawaii is the 50th state?

What is the state capital? The state flag? The seal? The state bird? The state flower?

The primary age student needs specific direction in completing research.

• Introduce the students to the state song.

Supplemental Activities

• The students would enjoy a field trip to the state capital. The capital rotunda will include pictures or statues of key individuals and events in the state's history. It may be possible for the student to see the legislature in session, or see original documents of the state constitution.

• Teach some basic ideas of flag etiquette.

• Look at the design of your state flag. What do each of the symbols represent?

• Research the many flags which have been part of the history of the United States.

CONCLUSION

1/2-1 Week

|  *Leading Idea* | ***History is His Story.*** |

- The Scriptures reveal the fact that God has been working in the lives of men and nations since the beginning of time.

Therefore, History is His Story or God's Story. History is the record of God working in the lives of men and nations.

For Reflection and Reasoning

- At the beginning of this year, we discussed why we study history. We want to "remember what God has done." From history class this year, what have you learned that "God has done?"

- Spend some time looking through the student's notebook to "remember" highlights of the year's study and to answer questions which will bring to the student's mind the key Ideas which were taught for each section of this year's study.

- How did history change when Christ came? Does Christ help us to govern our

actions? How?

- Why do we need the Bible to govern our own actions? Why did the people need a Bible before a nation like America could be started? Why do Americans today need to read and study the Bible if we are to keep our liberty?

- Why is it important for American Christians to study the history of the United States of America?

- Sing some songs which identify God's power and control. Examples: *I Sing the Mighty Power of God; And God Said; All Things Bright and Beautiful.*

Part IV

APPENDIX

Endnotes

[1] Emma Willard, *History of the United States, or Republic of America*, 1845, in *The Christian History of the Constitution of the United States of America: Christian Self-Government* (San Francisco: Foundation for American Christian Education, 1966), page 405.

[2] Rev. S. W. Foljambe, "The Hand of God in American History", 1876, in *The Christian History of the American Revolution: Consider and Ponder* (San Francisco: Foundation for American Christian Education, 1976), page 47.

[3] Rev. S. W. Foljambe, *The Christian History of the American Revolution: Consider and Ponder*, page 46.

[4] Verna M. Hall, *The Christian History of the Constitution of the United States of America: Christian Self-Government* (San Francisco: Foundation for American Christian Education, 1966), page 6A.

[5] Katherine Dang, "Geography: An American Christian Approach", *A Guide to American Christian Education for the Home and School* (Camarillo: American Christian History Institute, 1987), page 272.

[6] Rev. S. W. Foljambe, *The Christian History of the American Revolution: Consider and Ponder*, page 47.

[7] Arnold Guyot, *Physical Geography*, 1873. (Palo Cedro: American Christian History Institute), pages 119-121.

[8] Katherine Dang, *Universal History, Volume I: Ancient History—Law Without Liberty* (Oakland: Katherine Dang, 2000), page 8.

[9] Leonard Bacon, *Genesis of the New England Churches*, 1874, in *The Christian History of the Constitution of the United States of America: Christian Self-Government* (San Francisco: Foundation for American Christian Education, 1966), page 16.

[10] Philip Schaff, *History of the Christian Church, Volume III*. Reprint (A, P & A), pages 159, 245-247.

[11] H. W. Hoare, *The Evolution of the English Bible*, 1901, in *The Christian History of the Constitution of the United States of America: Christian Self-Government* (San Francisco: Foundation for American Christian Education, 1966), pages 30-31.

[12] J. H. Merle d'Aubigne, *The Reformation in England, Volume I*, 1853. (Carlisle: The Banner of Truth Trust, 1977), pages 398-399.

[13] J. H. Merle d'Aubigne, *The Reformation in England, Volume II*, 1853. (Carlisle: The Banner of Truth Trust, 1977), pages 346-347.

[14] H. W. Hoare, page 30.

[15] Kay Brigham, Trans., *Christopher Columbus's Book of Prophecies*, by Christopher Columbus (Fort Lauderdale: TSELF, Inc., 1992), pages 173-183.

[16] Rev. S. W. Foljambe, *The Christian History of the American Revolution: Consider and Ponder*, page 47.

[17] Verna M. Hall, *The Christian History of the American Revolution: Consider and Ponder* (San Francisco: Foundation for American Christian Education, 1976), page xxv.

[18] Washington Irving, *The Life and Voyages of Christopher Columbus, Volume I* (Chicago: Hooper, Clarke & Co.), page 14.

[19] William Robertson, *History of the Discovery and Settlement of America*, 1835, in *The Christian History of the Constitution of the United States of America: Christian Self-Government* (San Francisco: Foundation for American Christian Education, 1966), pages 156-157.

[20] Edward Arber, *The Settlement of Jamestown* (Boston: Old South Association), page 19.

21 Thomas Studley, Robert Fenton, Edward Harrington, and John Smith, *The Settlement of Jamestown* (Boston: Old South Association), pages 14-15.

22 Edward Arber, page 19.

23 Gilbert Burnet, D.D., as quoted in *The Christian History of the American Revolution: Consider and Ponder* (San Francisco: Foundation for American Christian Education, 1976), page xxix.

24 William Bradford, *Of Plimoth Plantation* (Boston: Wright & Potter Printing Co., 1901), pages 11-13.

25 Ibid., page 16.

26 Ibid., page 21.

27 Ibid., page 32.

28 Ibid., page 57.

30 Ibid., page 85.

31 Ibid., pages 94-97.

31 Ibid., page 109.

32 Ibid., pages 111-112.

33 Rosalie J. Slater, *Teaching and Learning America's Christian History* (San Francisco: Foundation for American Christian Education, 1965), page 123.

34 William Bradford, pages 114-115.

35 Ibid., page 162.

36 Ibid., page 162-164.

37 Ibid., pages 170-171.

38 Moses Coit Tyler, as quoted in *Teaching and Learning America's Christian History* (San Francisco: Foundation for American Christian Education, 1965), p. 89.

39 Daniel Webster, *The Works of Daniel Webster, Volume I* (Boston: Little, Brown and Company, 1856), page 150.

40 Washington Irving, *Life of George Washington, Volume I* (New York: G. P. Putnam's Sons, 1857), pages 45-52.

41 Ibid., pages 56-57.

42 "Hip-length leggins of skins and a sort of knee-length coat, belted at the waist, after the style of what became known as the 'hunting shirt' during the Revolutionary War."

43 "So called because made of skins that were matched in putting them together. There was a coarse woolen cloth known as 'match-cloth' which was used by the English in imitation of the Indian skin coat. It is, of course, impossible to say whether Washington's coat was of skins or cloth."

44 John C. Fitzpatrick, A.M., Editor, *The Diaries of George Washington, Volume I, 1748-1770* (Boston and New York: Houghton Mifflin Company, 1925), pages 43-67.

45 *The Papers of George Washington, Volume I* (Charlottesville: University Press of Virginia, 1983), pages 339-340.

46 Ibid., page 343.

47 Benson J. Lossing, *Cyclopædia of United States History, Volume II* (New York: Harper & Brothers, Publishers, 1892), page 1442.

48 *The Family Circle—1857*, in *The Christian History of the American Revolution: Consider and Ponder* (San Francisco: Foundation for American Christian Education, 1976), Frontispiece.

49 Henry Melchior Muhlenberg, as quoted in *The Christian History of the American Revolution: Consider and Ponder* (San Francisco: Foundation for American Christian Education, 1976), page 68.

50 Benson J. Lossing, *History of the United States,* 1860.

51 Emerson Hough, *The Way to the West,* (New York: Grosset & Dunlap, 1903), pages 88-89.

52 Ibid., page 96.

53 Ibid., pages 103-104.

54 Ibid., pages 105-106.

55 Cecil B. Hartley, *The Life of Daniel Boone* (New York: Grosset & Dunlap, 1900), p. 78.

56 Hough, pages 107-108.

57 Hartley, page 79.

58 Ibid., pages 330-332.

59 Ibid., pages 354-355.

60 Abraham Lincoln, Letter to J. W. Fell, December 20, 1859. *Abraham Lincoln From His Own Words and Contemporary Accounts* (Washington, D.C.: National Park Service, 1942), page 1.

61 William Wood's Statement to Herndon, September 15, 1865. *Abraham Lincoln From His Own Words and Contemporary Accounts* (Washington, D.C.: National Park Service, 1942), page 3.

62 Lincoln to J. W. Fell, page 2.

63 Mrs. Thomas Lincoln's Statement to Herndon, September 8, 1865. *Abraham Lincoln From His Own Words and Contemporary Accounts* (Washington, D.C.: National Park Service, 1942), page 43.

64 Lincoln to J. W. Fell, page 2.

65 William H. Herndon, *The Hidden Lincoln*, in *Abraham Lincoln From His Own Words and Contemporary Accounts* (Washington, D.C.: National Park Service, 1942), pages 44-45.

66 Lincoln to J. W. Fell, page 2.

67 Abraham Lincoln, Lincoln Springfield Speech, June 26, 1857. *Abraham Lincoln From His Own Words and Contemporary Accounts* (Washington, D.C.: National Park Service, 1942), pages 12-13.

68 Abraham Lincoln, Springfield Speech, June 16, 1858. *Abraham Lincoln From*

His Own Words and Contemporary Accounts (Washington, D.C.: National Park Service, 1942), pages 13-14.

69 Abraham Lincoln, Letter to Horace Greeley, August 22, 1862. *Abraham Lincoln From His Own Words and Contemporary Accounts* (Washington, D.C.: National Park Service, 1942), page 29.

70 Abraham Lincoln, Letter to A. G. Hodges, April 4, 1864. *Abraham Lincoln From His Own Words and Contemporary Accounts* (Washington, D.C.: National Park Service, 1942), pages 40-43.

71 Abraham Lincoln, Second Inaugural Address, March 4, 1865. *Abraham Lincoln From His Own Words and Contemporary Accounts* (Washington, D.C.: National Park Service, 1942), page 48.

72 *Teaching and Learning America's Christian History* (San Francisco: Foundation for American Christian Education, 1965), pages 262-263.

73 Rosalie J. Slater, *American Men of Science and Invention* (San Francisco: Foundation for American Christian Education).

74 James Madison, as quoted in *The Christian History of the Constitution of the United States of America: Christian Self-Government* (San Francisco: Foundation for American Christian Education, 1966), page 248A.

75 Samuel F. B. Morse, Letter to Sidney E. Morse, Esq., May 31, 1864. *The Samuel Finley Breese Morse Family Papers* (Washington, D.C.: Library of Congress).

76 Patricia Ryon Quiri, *Alexander Graham Bell* (New York: F. Watts, 1991).

77 Alexander Graham Bell, *Bell Family Papers* (Washington, D.C.: Library of Congress).

78 Felix Morley, *The Power in the People*, 1949, in *Teaching and Learning America's Christian History* (San Francisco: Foundation for American Christian Education, 1965), pages 206-207.

Bibliography

Appleman, Roy Edgar, Editor. *Abraham Lincoln From His Own Words and Contemporary Accounts.* Washington, D.C.: National Park Service, 1942.

Bell, Alexander Graham. *Bell Family Papers.* Washington, D.C.: Library of Congress.

Bradford, William. *Of Plimoth Plantation.* Boston: Wright & Potter Printing Co., 1901.

Brigham, Kay, Trans. *Christopher Columbus's Book of Prophecies,* by Christopher Columbus. Fort Lauderdale: TSELF, Inc., 1992.

Dang, Katherine. *Universal History, Volume I. Ancient History—Law Without Liberty.* Oakland: Katherine Dang, 2000.

D'Aubigne, J. H. Merle. *The Reformation in England, Volume I and II,* 1853. Carlisle: The Banner of Truth Trust, 1977.

Fitzpatrick, John C., Editor. *The Diaries of George Washington,* Vols. 1-5. The Mount Vernon Ladies' Association of the Union, 1925.

Gross, Ruth Belov. *True Stories about Abraham Lincoln.* New York: Lothrop, Lee & Shepard Books, 1973.

Guyot, Arnold. *Physical Geography.* Palo Cedro: American Christian History Institute.

Hall, Verna M. *The Christian History of the American Revolution: Consider and Ponder.* San Francisco: Foundation for American Christian Education, 1976.
The Christian History of the Constitution of the United States of America: Christian Self-Government. San Francisco: Foundation for American

Christian Education, 1966.

Hartley, Cecil B. *The Life of Daniel Boone.* New York: Grosset & Dunlap, 1900.

Henry, Matthew. *Exposition of the Old and New Testament.* London: James Nisbet & Co., Limited.

Hough, Emerson. *The Way to the West.* New York: Grosset & Dunlap, 1903.

Irving, Washington. *The Life and Voyages of Christopher Columbus.* Chicago: Hooper, Clarke & Co.
Life of George Washington, Vols. 1-5. New York: G. P. Putnam's Sons, 1857.

Kerby, Mona. *Samuel Morse.* New York: Franklin Watts, 1991.

Long, William J. *American Literature.* Chicago: Ginn and Company, 1923.

Lossing, Benson J. *Harpers' Popular Cyclopædia of United States History.* New York: Harper & Brothers, Publishers, 1892.
History of the United States. 1860.

Montgomery, D. H. *The Beginner's American History.* Boston: Ginn & Company, 1901

Morison, Samuel Eliot. *Admiral of the Ocean Sea.* Boston: Little, Brown, and Company, 1942.
Christopher Columbus, Mariner. New York: The New American Library, 1955.
Journals and Other Documents on the Life and Voyages of Christopher Columbus. New York: The Heritage Press, 1963.

Pollard, Josephine. *Christopher Columbus and the Discovery of the New World.* Granger: Pilgrim Institute, 1992.

Poole, Matthew. *A Commentary on the Holy Bible.* Mclean: MacDonald Publishing Company.

Quiri, Patricia Ryon. *Alexander Graham Bell.* New York: F. Watts, 1991.

Rose, James B. *A Guide to American Christian Education for the Home and School.* Camarillo: American Christian History Institute, 1987.

Sandburg, Carl. *Abe Lincoln Grows Up.* New York: Harcourt, Brace & World, Inc., 1956.

Schaff, Philip. *History of the Christian Church, Volume III.* Reprint A, P & A.

Slater, Rosalie J. *Teaching and Learning America's Christian History and Government: The Principle Approach.* San Francisco: Foundation for American Christian Education, 1965.

American Men of Science and Invention. San Francisco: Foundation for American Christian Education.

Smith, Captain John and Others. *The Settlement of Jamestown.* Old South Leaflets, No. 167. Boston: Old-South Association.

Smith, Jeanette K. and Ruth J. Smith. *An American Christian Approach for Teaching Christopher Columbus in the Primary Grades.* Granger: Pilgrim Institute, 1993.

Smith, Ruth J. "Teaching America's Christian History in the Elementary School." *A Guide to American Christian Education for the Home and School,* by James B. Rose. Palo Cedro: American Christian History Institute, 1987.

Steele, Joel Dorman and Esther Baker Steele. *Barnes's School History of the United States.* American Book Company, 1913.

Washington, George. *Papers of George Washington, The.* Charlottesville: University Press of Virginia, 1983.

Webster, Daniel. *The Works of Daniel Webster,* Volume I. Boston: Little, Brown and Company, 1856.

Webster, Noah. *An American Dictionary of the English Language.* 1828. Facsimile, San Francisco: Foundation for American Christian Education, 1967.

Webster's Biographical Dictionary. Springfield: G. & C. Merriam Co., Publishers, 1943.